P9-ARH-485

Russian Research Center Studies, 14

MARXISM

The Unity of Theory

and Practice

MARXISM
The Unity of Theory and Practice

A Critical Essay by Alfred G. Meyer

Reissued with a New Introduction

Harvard University Press · Cambridge

1970

335.4
M612m

© Copyright 1954 and 1970 by the President and Fellows of
Harvard College
Reissued, 1970

This volume was prepared under a grant from the Carnegie Corporation of New York. That Corporation is not, however, the author,
owner, publisher, or proprietor of this publication and is not to be
understood as approving by virtue of its grant any of the statements
made or views expressed therein.

The Russian Research Center of Harvard University is supported by
a grant from the Carnegie Corporation. The Center carries out interdisciplinary study of Russian institutions and behavior.

Distributed in Great Britain by
Oxford University Press, London

Library of Congress Catalog Card Number: 73–123568
SBN 674–55102–8
Printed in the United States of America

To the memory of my parents

North Carolina Wesleyan College Library
Rocky Mount, North Carolina 27801

14129

CONTENTS

INTRODUCTION, 1970

After almost twenty years, an author is bound to face one of his first books with ambivalence. He is likely to have learned more about the subject matter than he knew when he wrote the book. He may also have changed his style of writing, his approach, or indeed his total outlook on the world.

I shall try, in this new Introduction, to point out some of the things I have learned since writing this book, the text of which is here being reissued without revision. But I would first like to mention that some relevant external circumstances have changed as much as I have. This book was written in the period of McCarthyism, the period in which people like Stalin, Molotov, Adenauer, and Dulles were prominent, and in which the cold war as well as the hunt for heretics dominated politics. The Rosenbergs, Owen Lattimore, Alger Hiss, and the leaders of the Communist Party were tried in these years; and the accuser of Hiss was successful in his bid for the Vice-Presidency. The State Department was being purged of its China specialists, and the House Committee on Un-American Activities was making its inquisitorial visits to American universities. Anyone with aspirations to success in the academic world was well advised in those years to practice careful self-censorship when writing on a topic as politically suspect as Marxism; and I myself remember making changes in the manuscript on the advice of a friendly senior professor, who was to recommend the book for publication: he thought I sounded too sympathetic to Marxism in some passages. The basic premises of the cold war were then taken for granted by almost all Americans. Most of us studied the Soviet Union or "its" ideology for the sake of knowing the enemy, not for other reasons, and the highly controversial assumption that Marxism was "the ideology" of the Soviet Union was accepted as self-evident by almost everyone. I do not mean to underrate the scholars who were studying the Soviet Union in those years. On the contrary, they were doing pioneer work, and I am proud to have been associated with them. But the work was inevitably skewed, our interpretations distorted, by the cold-war environment within which we were all functioning.

Such an attitude was not propitious for the study of Marx and Marxism; and this topic was therefore suffering badly from neglect, philosophers, economists, sociologists, and political theorists tending to shrug Marx off as irrelevant — a mid-nineteenth century radical who had made much noise but contributed nothing of lasting significance. The Marx renaissance already under way in Western Europe at that time had made little impact in American academic circles. Of the lively debates over the humanist philosophy contained in Marx's early publications and drafts, the young American scholar was likely to learn only haphazardly. It seems to me that this neglect of Marx studies is reflected in my book, especially in the dearth of citations from some works considered significant today, but also in my failure to differentiate sufficiently between the ideas of Marx and those of Engels. If nonetheless a highly respected university press published it, that too reflects the low level of American marxology at the time; not that excellent studies were not available, but they were so little known in the academic world that a young scholar might not notice them — and get away with it.

Having said this, I shall not turn to a self-congratulatory survey of the progress we have made in this regard, although I do intend to say a few words, some pages below, about the impact of Marxism on contemporary social science and philosophy in the non-socialist world. Here, instead, let me outline briefly in what respects a book on Marxism, were I to write it today, would differ from the one I presented almost two decades ago.

At that time I sought to offer as systematic, integrated, and coherent a presentation of Marxism as possible, in a language that made sense to readers unfamiliar with Hegelian jargon. I still think that such an attempt is needed, but today I would balance it with somewhat increased emphasis on the many ambiguities inherent in Marxism and on the controversies they have engendered. Without an awareness of these ambiguities, the history of Marxism since the death of Marx cannot be understood. In line with this, I would have dwelled on the problem of defining the relationship between the Young Marx and the Mature Marx, or between his early philosophic writings and his later economic and political ones. A good case can be made for several positions here, and my own inclination would be to marshal all arguments and then leave the question unresolved. Further, I would have tried to bring out more carefully the specific contributions made to Marxism by Engels, and the important differences between Marx and Engels on some crucial philosophic questions. I shall discuss some of these differences toward the end of this essay. Here let me point out that a large portion of what for many decades was considered orthodox Marxism is in fact based on the writings of Engels and often is in conflict with the views of Marx.

Another matter I would stress today more than I did in the first edition is the continuity of Marxism with antecedent intellectual currents. For instance, Marx was very much a child (or grandchild) of the Enlightenment. He shared its critical spirit, especially its rejection of Christianity and all forms of thought control, its moral outcry against abuses of authority and privilege, as well as its suspicion of metaphysical speculation. His secularism, his materialism, and his faith in science were all echoes of eighteenth-century attitudes, as was his assumption that, fundamentally, men were rational beings who could fashion for themselves an ideal social order, hence that progress and freedom were attainable. Many ancient writers who were the culture heroes of the *philosophes* were heroes for Marx as well. Needless to say, this identification of Marx as a grandchild of the Enlightenment must be hedged in with serious qualifications. After all, he voiced some sharp criticism specifically of the XVIIIth-Century *philosophes*.

That Marx was profoundly indebted also to Romanticism, I stressed in the original book. But it might have been interesting to point out that he drew some important ideas not only from Rousseau and from the Rousseauian spirit of criticizing modern civilization, but also — indirectly — from some of the most conservative critics of Liberalism, such as Bonald and de Maistre, whose attacks on the results of the French Revolution and on the philosophy of Liberalism anticipated some of the positions of revolutionary socialism, just as de Maistre's critique of liberal thinking anticipated a good deal of Marx's theory of ideology. At the same time, the influence which socialist precursors, the so-called Utopians, had on Marx should have been stressed, especially that of Saint-Simon, this influential thinker who so much eludes our attempts to place him on the right or the left extreme of the political spectrum. In expressing the belief that I have belittled their influence on Marx or simply paid insufficient attention to them, I am reflecting the increased attention which students of intellectual history have been paying the Utopian Socialists lately. They are being rediscovered partly because ours is a time in which utopian thought is once again becoming fashionable or relevant. Of course, when more attention is paid to all the intellectual currents mentioned so far, the relationship of Marx to his closer antecedents, Hegel and the Hegelian Left, must also receive more stress, and with it the entire German scene before and after the revolutions of 1848, and the broader panorama of mid-nineteenth-century European politics and culture. All these connecting links are discussed far more intensively today than they were when I wrote this book.

One connection, however, to which I would also pay far more attention is still disregarded almost as much as it was fifteen or twenty years ago. That is the Judaeo-Christian heritage. And I must say a few words about its impact on the theories of Marx and Engels.

Most broadly speaking, this heritage underlies all Western thought of the last thousand years; and much of it is contained in the Enlightenment, which, with its anti-Christian bias, might be characterized as secularized Christianity, or counter-Christianity — in any event, a Christian heresy. The men of the Enlightenment, and also its grandchildren, like Marx, were preoccupied with the salvation of mankind. They saw history as a drama with a foreordained happy conclusion. In great moral seriousness, most starkly exemplified by Kantian rigorism, they stressed the individual's responsibility in playing his destiny-given role: they were preoccupied with the existence of evil and with the effort to overcome and subdue it. In addition, they were interested in metaphysical and ontological questions regarding the nature of reality and the origins of the universe. Carl Becker, among others, has pointed out how similar the questions asked by the *philosophes* were to the questions posed by the scholastics; and the same questions reappear in Marxism.

Marx and Engels themselves were steeped in Judaeo-Christian ideas by upbringing, intellectual training, and the philosophic climate of their youth. In becoming convinced atheists, anthropocentrists, and enemies of religion, they represent both the Enlightenment and mid-nineteenth-century radicalism. But, in observing this, one must be aware that, psychologically speaking, both men — Marx much more than Engels — paid a heavy price for this conversion; in the depth of their souls they do not seem ever to have quite emancipated themselves. The very vehemence of their attacks on Judaism and Christianity betrays this, and so do the frequent allusions to religious literature in their writings. These allusions are part of the style in which people wrote in those decades; but beyond that Marx showed ironic awareness of the many parallels between his own and Christian theories. It is these parallels I would like to discuss at this point, and for this purpose I propose to examine the philosophic core of all Marxist theories — the dialectic.

In the work published almost two decades ago, I felt that I had done an adequate job of explaining the dialectic. I interpreted it to be a not quite successful attempt to develop an ontology of complexity, process, conflict, and development, laudable in its intent, useful as a heuristic device, but easily misunderstood because of its cumbersome and inadequate vocabulary, and because of its developers' recklessness in tearing down the boundaries between discrete areas of philosophic inquiry. I stand by this interpretation still today, but I would add that it is not a complete rendition of the dialectic; in fact, it misses its essence as I understand it today: I had missed the religious kernel it contains. Once that kernel is recognized, the dialectic appears as a secularized theodicy.

Theodicy is that branch of theology which seeks to cope with the existence of evil. Anyone who believes in a god who is the epitome of all desirable human qualities — the ultimate in goodness, wisdom, and power — must be puzzled by the universal prevalence of inequity and suffering in the world of man. Given an all-mighty, all-kind, and all-foreseeing god, how can one explain the misery of human existence? Did God plan it that way, for whatever purpose? If so, he seems an evil god, not a good one. Did he make mistakes, did something go wrong with his creation, did he lose control? In that case he obviously is not all-mighty. Did he lose interest? Is he playing games with us? A positive answer to any one of these questions will undermine the faith in the Judaeo-Christian deity. The puzzle of evil, and the attempt to justify God, have therefore been among the most troublesome problems for theologians. And the problem reappears when Christianity is transformed into secular philosophies in which the deity is replaced by some abstraction such as the spirit of reason; and it reoccurs even in those "materialistic" or Promethean philosophies that see man as the sovereign demiurge of history.

The dialectic is one such attempt at theodicy. Its central preoccupation is with the mystery of a creativity in which good and evil, progress and retrogression, growth and decay, love and hate, life and death, merge and mingle and become part and consequence of each other.

In its strictly religious form, the dialectic is related to Manichaean and Gnostic heresies as well as to the ideas of many Christian mystics. Briefly, it defines creation as an eternal process in which God is objectified (reified, externalized, alienated): In the act or process of creation, God turns into objects, or parts of God are objectified. The objective world is therefore a reification of the divinity. It shares his divinity, but does so only inadequately or partly. The world of objects is both divine and less than divine, both God and not-God. In the act of creation, God therefore creates things external, foreign, indeed hostile, to himself; and in facing his creations, he confronts himself as something external and other. The creations are the creator at odds with himself, the (sovereign) subject become object.

Creation thus backfires on the creator. After the act of creation, there is tension in the world, and forever after all creation strains for relief of this tension. In Christian terminology: the aim of history is atonement, the return of all creation to God. Translated into secular philosophy, this mystical goal of St. Thomas à Kempis becomes the merger of subject and object or the resolution of all alienation. All dualism is alienation — the dualism of male and female, life and death, community and society, nature and reason, body and soul, matter and spirit, "is" and "ought." To the dialectician these and other dichotomies are false and must be overcome, just as the rigid boundaries between philosophic categories are false and must be broken down. And the only way the dialectician knows to reverse alienation is by intensifying it. He seems confident that evils, when driven to intolerable intensity, will turn into their opposites. Fire will be fought with fire; poison will turn into medicine; through our sins as much as despite them we will receive grace — ideas of this kind in which evil becomes a blessing are as old as magic itself, and the subject of countless myths. Christian thought is replete with this belief in the reversal of the dialectic of evil. The original sin, by which man rebelled against his creator, was to eat of the fruit from the tree of knowledge; but salvation, too, will come from knowledge, albeit a higher one. The notion of conflict resolution on some higher level recurs in all dialectical philosophy. We have to die in order to live eternally. By man came death, but by man came also the resurrection of the dead. And so forth. In contemporary political ideology the same notion is expressed by Frantz Fanon, who argues that the black victim of violence must purge himself of the resultant dehumanization by first indulging in an orgy of counter-violence.

Similarly, in Marx, the original sin of production (Marx himself used this terminology) will lead to freedom from material concerns, hence by implication to a more spiritual man; misery will lead to revolution and deliverance from misery, and ideology will turn into consciousness. All past social systems fall because their very accomplishments hasten their internal contradictions; yet all the evils of the past will disappear because they themselves hasten the disappearance of evil. The dialectic, seen in this light, is a consoling faith in salvation by predetermination, a faith intensified by the very depth of depravity into which man has fallen. All history marches toward the fulfillment of a promise God seems well nigh to have forgotten.

In Hegel's philosophy, Christian doctrines are secularized, or, better perhaps, intellectualized. God is transformed into the absolute spirit, the spirit of reason, or the spirit of freedom. God becomes rationality and autonomy. All history is the objectification and externalization of this absolute spirit. Historic events and social institutions are all objective manifestations of the absolute — part of it and external to it — sharing its rationality, but sharing it inadequately. All objective phenomena are not quite reasonable, but strain toward reasonability.

The dialectic here is a pattern of creation, in which the subject (the spirit of reason) is objectified, or objectifies himself, through successive stages, a process of "unfolding," where the final goal is reunification or reconciliation, the object returning to the subject — in Hegel, reason returning to itself. Reason returns to itself when the objects acquire consciousness, i.e., when the objects know themselves as rational or reasonable, when the world knows itself as divine. The fruit of the tree of knowledge alienates, but also makes him who eats it like God. Hegel believed in salvation through philosophy, even while he acknowledged that philosophy has alienated man from creation.

Hegel refers to the goal of all creation as self-actualization. Each thing strives to realize all that it is potentially. This, he argues, takes place easily in natural organisms; for nature is wise. But it is complicated in the realm of the spirit, i.e., in human history, because spirit, taking the form of human consciousness and human will, complicates things. Hegel echoes Rousseau's essay on the origins of inequality among men, where Rousseau argues that intellectual activity, the specifically human quality, alienates man from nature. "The spirit," writes Hegel, "is at war with itself. It has to overcome itself as the most serious obstacle." This contradictory nature of the human spirit of reason becomes the basic explanation for the unspeakable misery of human history. Humanity is reasonable as well as unreasonable. Will clashes against will, passion against passion, ignorance against ignorance. All of these are manifestations of the spirit of reason; hence the absolute spirit objectifies himself as stupidity and cruelty, and all human history is suffering. But the ultimate reasonability of the spiritual demiurge guarantees a happy outcome; and for Hegel the ultimate destiny of mankind is freedom. Just as the Christian god is full of tricks, so Hegel's reason uses cunning.

Feuerbach and Marx inverted this dialectic. For them the subject of history, i.e., the creator, is neither God nor an abstract spirit of reason or freedom. The subject is the human species. Echoing the Sophists, Feuerbach points out that man, the creator, creates God in his own image, investing this fiction with all the best qualities and potentialities he himself possesses, but in this process robbing himself of some of these potentialities. The creation of God is therefore, for Feuerbach, the basic act of alienation and externalization. Man has projected his own potential for creativity, autonomy, and fulfillment onto an artifact, a fetish, and by this act alienated his happiness. Man, the highest being, has forfeited his sovereignty. God becomes alienated humanity; and religion becomes man's alienated happiness and fulfillment. To reverse this fall from grace, Feuerbach suggests that man realize religion as the alienation it is, that he become conscious of himself as the sovereign of history. To this Marx adds the important, nay critical, step of arguing that such a change in consciousness by itself is insufficient to de-alienate man. Instead, a change in consciousness must be integrated with practical activity, with action. Mere contemplation is impotent; the task is to change the world. The dualism of theory and practice is the ultimate key to alienation; hence the fundamental task is to overcome this dualism.

Marx took an additional step: he applied Feuerbach's reversal of the Hegelian dialectic to all human activities, not just religion, but primarily economics and politics, and secondarily to all other pursuits. He also made it historical and concrete. His highest being, or subject, is man, who has created himself, and who, by exercising his creativity, has created forces seemingly beyond his control. He now lives an alienated life. His labor is alienated creativity; his ideologies are alienated consciousness; his family life is alienated sexuality; his political life is alienated sovereignty. (Marx might have added that man's art is alienated play. But he never managed to incorporate his ideas concerning art into the framework of his more general theories.)

This down-to-earth dialectic preserves the basic idea of the Christian and Hegelian dialectics — creativity as a disturbance of a natural harmony, disturbing because it means the objectification and alienation of the subject. As in the religious version, so in Marx the loss of self — alienation — is implied already in the first step of creation, or self-creation; but it is spelled out more clearly in paradise (primitive communism) when man has begun to eat from the tree of knowledge and become productive.

In the religious dialectic, God created for six days, making something more marvelous every day, in every step creating something more divine than what the previous day had brought forth. And on the last day he created a being in his very own image, which would be able to appreciate and admire all previous handiwork and would sing the praise of the creator. But this articulate being disobeyed, wanting to assume control. In the Marxian dialectic, man is the creator who appropriates nature and makes it his own by re-making it, so as to liberate himself from natural necessity. But production alienates; or, rather, it is alienation: what man creates for himself is objectification of his own self; in the objects he has made he confronts his own reifications, his own self as a hostile force. And this dialectical drama takes place anew in every period of history, because the very techniques and human relations which bring success to a new social system will also, inevitably, cause it to fall.

As I have presented it here, the dialectic is more than an ontology of complexity, process, and change, although it contains such an ontology within itself. Beyond that, however, it is a form of philosophizing about the puzzle of creation, the metabolic relationship between man and his environment, and the fateful unity-in-opposition of being and consciousness, thought and action. It muses about the fact that all human action has unpredictable and unintended consequences, that one cannot act without making grave mistakes. It is thus preoccupied with the inevitability of sin and evil and is therefore of one piece with religious thought even when it tries to substitute secular for religious terminology. It certainly appeals to man's religious and aesthetic senses as much as to the sociologist's or economist's cognitive aims. Indeed, it is as much poetry as it is science and logic. Being poetry, it makes sense to some and not to others, but is not subject to empirical validation.

What explains my late discovery of this meaning in the Marxian dialectic? One possible explanation is suggested in the preceding paragraph: perhaps I was not sufficiently attuned to the poetry in Marx, Hegel, and preceding systems of thought. Certainly, once he is attuned to it, anyone reading Marx will encounter this poetry in every major work of his. He will meet it as specific ideas, and he will see it take form in Marx's style of writing, with its love for ambivalence and pun, and its predilection for reversing subject and predicate — joining the weapon of criticism to the criticism of weapons, or reviewing Proudhon's *Philosophy of Poverty* as the poverty of philosophy. In the "mature" Marx, to be sure, the language of the dialectic often appears to be little more than a stylistic device, even a mannerism, whereas in the earlier works contradiction and the reversal of subject and object, or subject and predicate, are philosophic categories. Moreover, words like alienation and externalization are used more rarely, though even in *Das Kapital* the concept of fetishism looms large.

Still, one can discern a tendency in Marx, which is stronger in Engels and stronger yet in their immediate followers: it is a tendency to shy away from religious terminology, from grand philosophic generalities, from all moralizing, and from poetic imagery. Under Engels and his "orthodox" disciples, the emphasis was increasingly laid on science and materialism. And from the poetry of creativity the dialectic was transformed into the ontology of process. It is that dialectic which I summarized in the book now being reissued. As a consequence, the treatment of many related themes appears to me today to have been shallow or, as dialecticians might say, undialectical.

Today some of my undergraduates are able to point out the defects of my interpretation. What explains their improved insight? Obviously, a more sophisticated understanding of the dialectic is generally accepted and can be found, in one form or other, in a large number of books dealing with Marx. The growth of this better understanding is customarily explained by the publication of an unfinished manuscript on which Marx worked in 1844, the famous Economic-Philosophic Manuscript. In this fragment, Marx has some profound and very puzzling things to say about the alienation of labor and its resolution in communism. The work is the most important source for the interpretation of the dialectic offered here.

I do not find it plausible that the publication of this manuscript in German in 1932 is responsible for our changed interpretation of Marxism. After all, other works by Marx and Engels were available in which similar thoughts were expressed; and there were followers of Marx who even without access to these works or to the 1844 manuscript had interpreted Marx in thoroughly dialectical fashion, foremost among them György Lukács, who had come out with very similar views in 1923. Yet the work of Lukács was either not understood or was regarded as a departure from Marxist traditions. Moreover the publication of the 1844 manuscript made its impact only on a small handful of Marx specialists, whose writings in turn tended to be ignored; a book like Herbert Marcuse's *Reason and Revolution* was widely read only years after its first publication. Indeed, the 1844 manuscripts were published in English translation only about twenty-five years after they had first appeared in the original German. This delay in the impact made by the manuscript is the thing that has to be explained, not the impact itself.

The key to this delayed influence seems to me to be ideological. Theories of alienation have suddenly become fashionable. The Age of Longing, about which I spoke in the last chapter of this book, has descended upon us with far greater poignancy than I could have guessed twenty years ago. Similarly, radicalism has once again become much more meaningful and a much more widely accepted stance than it was when this book was first written. All this means that Marxism in its original apocalyptic meaning, with its philosophic-religious undertones of despair leading to hope, has acquired far greater plausibility — at least for those sharing this mood — than it has ever had. Moreover, once radicalism becomes a prevalent mood, radical thought must be studied also by the spokesmen for other moods. Compared to the present, the period in which this book was first written was a period of complacency, whereas ours is a troubled age. In such an age, one cannot be a philosopher or social scientist without taking the Marxian contribution into account. Hence, quite independently of the publication of this or that philosophic fragment, the writer whom my professors dismissed as a negligible crank twenty years ago is today studied more intensively than perhaps any other intellectual figure from the nineteenth century, with the possible exception of Nietzsche.

It should now be clear, however, that the Marx who is studied today, in the West as well as in Eastern Europe, is different from the Marx (to say nothing about the Engels) whom I have quoted in this book. He is as radical as I have described him. But he is a bit less of an empiricist than I have made him out to be; indeed, he called himself a humanist rather than a materialist, quite in tune with his anthropocentric theodicy; and he is quite a bit less optimistic than some of my readers take him to be on the basis of this book. The dialectic dwells on the persistence of evil as much as on the underlying rationality, on the tragedy of human existence as much as on the prospect of salvation, on the jokes which history plays on us as much as on the Promethean image of man.

The current Marx renaissance is therefore to some extent a symptom of doubt and despair; it expresses feelings of disgust, moral outrage, sardonic humor, and general alienation. It appeals to those who harbor serious doubts about the viability of established social systems and yet are unwilling to relinquish a well-ingrained faith in ultimate progress. In particular, it attracts those who pin their confidence on the principal victims of contemporary societies — workers, ghetto dwellers, peasants; the young, the poor, the outcast. This renewed ideological affinity with Marxism is the basis for the intense preoccupation during the last decade or two with the scattered and obscure philosophic heritage of Marx; it accounts also for the continual dialog between Marxian and non-Marxian philosophers, including theologians. This dialog, too, has now gone on for about two decades.

In the course of this running debate, which is being conducted in a friendly and earnest spirit, it has become apparent that Marxian modes of thinking have penetrated far more deeply into Western thought or, better perhaps, that Western thought has far greater affinities to certain aspects of Marxism than has been assumed in the past. Many bits and pieces from the Marxian structure of ideas fit into other structures as well. I have tried to show this, among other things, by showing the identity of dialectical and functional thought. I could have added to this that most contemporary social scientists are determinists of some sort, at least to the extent of seeking to uncover connections between discrete societal sub-systems. That politics and economics are interdependent, or that kinship patterns, culture, education, and a host of other segments of social life are to some extent dependent on the social structure and the prevailing level of technology — such assumptions, once criticized as Marxian and therefore suspect, today seem self-evident to vast numbers of social scientists. Similarly, most of us take it for granted that it is useful to see societies as stratified, and in this connection one is no longer identified as a Marxist automatically if he operates with the concept of class and class structure. Much of contemporary sociology, in fact, is unthinkable without the influence of Marx. The very questions asked by the major pioneers of sociology in our century — Weber, Durkheim, Pareto, Mannheim, to name a few — were suggested by Marx or his followers; and entire branches of sociology, from stratification theories to the sociology of knowledge, art, and religion, significantly echo Marxian views.

In pointing this out, one must differentiate sharply between the absorption of selected Marxian views and the acceptance of the total doctrine. Once this distinction is made it becomes clear that, on the whole, Marxism has been accepted piecemeal; and, if I was correct in defining it as a totality, in which each attitude supports and reinforces the other, then piecemeal acceptance is non-acceptance. Ideas taken out of the context in which they were embedded themselves undergo change. Concepts of stratification or group conflict separated from the Marxian theory of revolution differ from Marx's notion of the class struggle, and the sociology of knowledge differs from the Marxian theory of ideology. The contemporary social scientist is able to use bits and pieces from Marx's vocabulary and ideas because he can safely use them in his own intellectual pursuits. From the edifice of Marxism, the contemporary social scientist can pick numerous bricks with which to build structures of his own — if indeed we can speak about structures at all. Much social science today abhors grand theory of any kind. It concentrates instead on the individual stones and attempts to polish each one individually into a factual or methodological gem. It spurns attempts to place these gems into a diadem of knowledge about man, his history, or his institutions. In this, the behavioral social scientist resembles the modern artist whose aim seems to be to make any one technique or artistic device yield a maximum of effect in portraying a mood or solving some other aesthetic problem. Here, too, many of the devices and methods have been pioneered by the classical masters; but in their artistic work the methods were no more than the means for creating a much larger whole, bricks with which to build ambitious structures. In modern art as in contemporary social science, the fashioning of the bricks has become an end in itself. Studies are detailed and unconnected. This is, of course, as opposed to Marxism as it could possibly be.* The gap between Marxism and establishment social science is as great as before — and establishment social science here includes social science as practiced in the socialist countries. It is only on the fringes of the intellectual community in both East and West that the Marx renaissance has any meaning.

I have shown this little essay to a number of my students. The variety of reactions has surprised me a bit; it is amazing how many different things can be read into, or out of, seemingly simple prose. Of course, the prose is not simple at all; or if it is, the simplicity is deceptive, because the material it treats is slippery, poetic — dialectical. Nor should the variety of reactions to it have surprised me in the least, because that has happened before. A Spanish translation of this book could, for a number of years, and perhaps even now, be purchased wherever left-wing book-

---

* In this paragraph I repeat thoughts expressed in my "Marxism and Contemporary Social Science," *Centennial Review*, III, 4 (Fall 1959), pp. 433–434.

stores or outlets existed in Latin America; around 1960 it was the Fidelistas who were selling my book. Obviously they were unaware that the translation had been made at the suggestion, or with the support, of the United States Information Agency. Somebody must be fooling himself.

INTRODUCTION, 1954

One-fifth of the earth's land masses is ruled by a political system that traces its official ethos to the writings of Karl Marx and Friedrich Engels. In many other parts of the world, Marxist aims, Marxist programs for action, and Marxist methods of social science are discussed, pro and con, in heated controversies. For the last fifty-odd years, at least, our social scientists have, more and more, felt themselves compelled to take cognizance of this rebel school of social theory and deal with it one way or another.

There exists an overwhelming wealth of literature on Marxism written by, and for, the initiated, by, and for, men who have spent the whole or greater part of their adult lives in the study of Marxist writings, in the company of fellow-devotees, and in the common pursuit of Marxist objectives. It has, however, proven difficult for such people to communicate to those not initiated without either talking down to them in a patronizing tone or becoming dogmatic. Where the works of these life-long devotees do not take the form of catechisms, it is usually impossible for the layman to understand the really serious writings of the initiated because too much knowledge of Marxism is already taken for granted in them, basic terms remain undefined, and a fundamental agreement on an over-all view is presupposed.

Works on the part of non-Marxists, on the other hand, have often been based on misunderstanding or outright misinformation concerning Marxist theories, a failing that can to a considerable degree be laid at the doorstep of Marx and his followers themselves, who failed to present their doctrine in a systematic fashion and often stressed some parts of their work, neglecting very significant portions of Marx's writings. Moreover, the highly controversial nature of the theme has too often led to an undue predominance of criticism over information. Preconceptions and clichés, blind hostility and blind orthodoxy alike, have distorted the contours of Marxist thought.

One type of work on Marxism is almost entirely lacking. This is a study of the subject which attempts to go even slightly below the surface of the written word: a study which sets itself the aim of explaining the Marxist terminology in modern and accepted terms; of searching for the ideas and images that are represented by this terminology; of explaining, furthermore, the connections and coherences that have not been made explicit by Marx and his followers themselves; and, finally, of probing for the unexpressed attitudes, preconceptions, and traditions, psychological and ideological, that underly the entire thought structure. It is such a *Gestalt* view (if we may usurp this term) of Marxist ideas which this work tries to present, albeit in the sketchiest possible outline. We shall see that Marxism cannot be understood merely as a set of propositions concerning the nature of the universe or of society. Instead, we have to examine the propositions of Marxist social science in the light of certain political or moral attitudes which we shall characterize by the word *radicalism*, and also of certain hopes or beliefs, which give Marxism an essentially *optimistic* flavor. Our thesis is that these various elements are expressed by a great number of propositions which constitute the descriptive part of Marxist theory. We shall, further, note that these various elements of Marxism, or the implications drawn from them, may come into conflict, and that such conflicts are a more serious challenge to Marxist theory in its entirety than all the many intellectual errors and inconsistencies on which most critics dwell. True, the keystone of the Marxist structure of ideas is formed by an ingenious attempt to reconcile the contradictions and inconsistencies. We shall give an exposition of this attempt, examine its validity, and trace the consequences that occur when this validity is challenged.

The task of writing an introduction to Marxist thought is exceedingly difficult. The very vastness of the topic seems to prevent anyone but a life-long devotee from acquiring as thorough a knowledge of the literature as would be required for full understanding; and the sketchy treatment, in essay style, which has been given it here, betrays the fragmentary character of the author's knowledge. Moreover, this study was undertaken with more than one aim in mind, and the different purposes may sometimes have been at odds. The work is meant to be a critique of Marxist thought, not just a description. Yet, before a school of thought can be criticized it must be studied, and the critic must be extremely careful to give his readers all possible opportunity to study it objectively. This calls for studied and deliberate fairness on the part of the critic. However adverse his conclusions, he must give the ideology he criticizes a chance to defend itself. He must not only familiarize the reader with the various aspects of the ideological structure, he must also try to make these parts into as coherent and meaningful a totality as he can, giving the theory the fairest possible chance to convey a message. Hence, whenever there is doubt in his mind as to the significance or relevancy of certain statements made by the advocates of the theory, he must give these statements the benefit of the doubt by searching for the best possible sense they might make. His task is therefore, from the very beginning, a double one: He must first make an exposition and criticize only afterwards. He should be both defense and prosecutor; and in a certain sense, he must also assume the role of the judge and the jury.

A further difficulty is created by the fact that there really is no such thing as Marxism, clear and simple. As in the case of other isms, there are many conflicting schools which contend for the honor of being the orthodox heirs of the movement's founder. Partisans of every color, within and without the Marxist camp, have constructed their image of Marxism, often selecting one set of statements more or less arbitrarily, or even making up yet another, and proclaiming it to be "what Marx really meant." Since Marx cannot personally decide which of his interpreters has understood him best, everyone who wishes to present his thoughts is indeed compelled to undertake his own interpretation. Hence, every work on Marx should really be entitled *What Marx Means to Me*. Thus also, the present essay cannot but be a very personal interpretation of Marxist thought, based on the life and writings of Karl Marx, and, to a certain extent, of his friend, Friedrich Engels.[1] Frequently, reference is made in this work to Marxists in general. In such cases, the reader need not worry what type of Marxist is meant; what is referred to is either some statement or interpretation generally accepted by all those who call themselves followers of Marx, or else some issue which has remained obscure and therefore led to disputes within the Marxist camp. Though it may be important to know about these problems, it is not always necessary to state how various factions proposed to solve them.

That this kind of treatment leads to overgeneralization and neglect of detail is acknowledged. A book of this size can present but a sketchy outline of the ideas developed by a century-old movement, or even by one man. Hence it becomes necessary to pick out those of his ideas which appear most significant, a decision involving the writer's judgment. Moreover, this way of stating Marx's ideas all but neglects to take into account that these ideas did not spring out of his brain in fixed completeness. Marx, as any other thinker, changed his mind; and his writings, therefore, present a story of intellectual development. One aspect of this has been treated well by Sidney Hook, who, in his *From Hegel to Marx*, traces the steps by which young Marx turned, as it were, into a Marxist. But no one has yet written an exhaustive ideological analysis of Marx's intellectual development, that is, an account of the changes in his outlook, interests, and opinions, seen in the light of changes in his circumstances, political struggles, and other personal motives. In truly Marxist spirit, Karl Korsch writes:

With Marx and Engels, as indeed with most writers on the field of social, historical, political thought, books have not only a history of their own, but those histories of books — their times and conditions of birth, their addressees, their very titles, and their further adventures in new editions, translations, etc. — form an inseparable part of the history of the theories themselves. It is, therefore, a deplorable fact that hitherto not only the bourgeois critics of the so-called "Marxian contradictions" but even the most faithful adherents of Marx's materialistic science should have quoted his divers theoretical statements without reference to time, addressees, and other historical indices necessary for their materialistic interpretation. This "orthodox" procedure of quoting Marx's [or even Marx's and Engels'] statements quite in the abstract, just as the schoolmen quoted the words of Aristotle or the bible, is quite inadequate for a theoretical study of a given social theory from an historical and materialistic standpoint.[2]

The writer acknowledges the pertinence of this criticism. Indeed, no complete understanding of Marx's ideas can even be approximated without an awareness of their history. At the same time he considers it entirely legitimate to disregard the warning quoted above, as long as the scope of the present work is limited.

The image of Marxism presented here has been further shaped — and perhaps distorted — by the circumstances under which this study was undertaken. From an interest in Marx and Engels, the writer soon shifted to a study of Russian Communism and wrote his doctoral dissertation on "Lenin's Theory of Revolution." While attempting to prepare this doctoral thesis for publication, he came to feel that no fruitful work on Lenin was possible for him before he had clarified his thinking on the broad ideological heritage with which Lenin started out. Hence, the attempt at self-orientation which resulted from this, taking the form of the present work, is, in effect, a prolegomena to the study of Communist thought. This not only affected the choice of authors that were read in preparing this work, but may also have distorted the entire presentation of Marxism made therein. Yet, as long as this is stated at the outset, it may be entirely legitimate. It certainly does not mean that Lenin is the only possible or the only "true" Marxist, or that the Russian Bolsheviks have a monopoly on interpreting Marx. It does mean that a critique of Marxism which wants to retain modest scope might quite fruitfully be a critique of Marxism seen primarily as the ideological heritage on which Leninism is based.

Even with this qualification, the present work cannot by any means claim to cover this ideological heritage with any degree of thoroughness. It does not, for instance, undertake to criticize such concepts as "petty-bourgeoisie" or "Asiatic society," or the Marxist attitude to the peasantry, even though these aspects of Marx's ideas have turned out to be of particular relevance to

Russian developments. Nor does it deal with some of the economic concepts, such as the theory of value, the acceptance of which by Soviet economists has created such difficulties for Soviet planners.[3] Finally, this work contains no treatment of Marx as a political strategist; notable for its absence is a discussion of his relationship with Bakunin and the Anarchist movement, which is also of great interest to students of Russian Marxism, because Marx's affirmation of the proletarian dictatorship was to find a particularly strong echo in Russia.

PART I

EXPOSITION

Chapter One

The Marxist Contribution to Contemporary Social Science

> *. . . to show, by rigid scientific investigation, the necessity of successive determinate orders of social conditions, and to establish, as impartially as possible, the facts that serve him for fundamental starting points. For this it is quite enough if he proves, at the same time, both the necessity of the present order of things and the necessity of another order into which the first must inevitably pass over; and this all the same whether men believe or do not believe it, whether they are conscious or unconscious of it. Marx treats the social movement as a process of natural history, governed by laws not only independent of human will, consciousness, and intelligence, but rather, on the contrary, determining that will, consciousness, and intelligence.* Karl Marx[1]

Materialism, Free Will, and Determinism

Marx and Engels claimed that their theory was the last word in social science. No other view of society, they thought, could rival theirs in scientific exactness and reliability. No other theory, they asserted, was as faithful a reflection of reality as theirs.

This claim could not be supported even a hundred years ago. The Marxist view of the world is one in which certain crucial features of our age are highlighted and explained, features which other theories may leave in the dark or perceive through blurred spectacles. In that sense, Marxism has made undeniable contributions to social science. But it has faults and flaws and blind spots of its own which are no less serious than those of rival theories. The present work will trace the intellectual traditions, the underlying premises and attitudes that are at the root of these flaws. And we shall then examine how the structure of Marxist ideas fell apart as the inadequacies in the underpinnings became apparent. That is the purpose of this book.

In spite of this, we must not lose sight of any sound social science in its theories. Some of these contributions are hidden in a forbidding, esoteric jargon; and it will be our task to translate this lingo into common-sense language. Other important elements of Marxist social science were quickly forgotten or for a long time remained altogether undiscovered by other social scientists because they were so intimately linked with a rebel doctrine and a revolutionary movement. To summarize these contributions, and to give an image of Marx and Engels as among the pioneers of contemporary social science, will be the purpose of the present chapter. After taking this step, we shall be able to recognize the inadequacies of Marxism all the more clearly.

In claiming scientific validity for their theories, Marx and Engels thought of themselves as the last progeny of an impressive lineage of social scientists who, they thought, had made proper steps in the right direction even if they had not got hold of the entire truth. Among those who ranked particularly high in their estimation were Machiavelli and, even more so, Thomas Hobbes. They praised them for the "materialism" of their approach, claiming that "materialism" is one of the indispensable methods of social analysis. Their own theory, too, they said, was a materialistic theory.

It is easy to repeat this statement. It is more difficult to determine what it means. As commonly used, the word "materialism" has a number of distinct meanings; and even if we knew what these various meanings are, we should still have to find out whether Marx and Engels themselves had all these meanings — or any of them — in mind when they called their own theories "materialistic." People often use conventional terms in rather unconventional fashion, and we shall have to see whether Marx and Engels did not, perhaps, indulge in this confusing habit too.

At the funeral of Karl Marx, Engels, in his eulogy, praised his late friend for having proven conclusively that mankind must first eat and drink, have shelter and clothing, before it can pursue politics, religion, science, art, and so forth.[2] For the time being, in other words, the narrowest material problem of satisfying basic consumers' wants is highest on the agenda of mankind. This assertion of Marxism is, to many people, the very essence of Marx's materialism; and, true enough, Engels correctly stated his friend's theories. At the same time, the statement he made expresses only part of the Marxist idea. The aim which Marxist socialism hopefully envisages is the liberation of mankind from just this materialist pursuit. Material wants are regarded as an obstacle to be overcome before man can use his intelligence to make a more truly human history. Thus Marx asserted that ". . . the realm of freedom does not commence until the point is passed where labor under the compulsion of necessity and of external utility is required. In the very nature of things it lies beyond the sphere of material production in the strict meaning of the term. Just as the savage must wrestle with nature, in order to satisfy his wants, in order to maintain his life and reproduce it, so civilized man has to do it, and he must do it in all forms of society and under all possible modes of production. With his development the realm of natural necessity expands, because his wants increase; but at the same time the forces of production increase, by which these wants are satisfied. The freedom in this field cannot consist of anything else but of the fact that socialized man, the associated producers, regulate their interchange with nature rationally, bring it under their common control, instead of being ruled by it as by some blind power; that they accomplish their task with the least expenditure of energy and under conditions most adequate to their human nature and most worthy of it. But it always remains a realm of necessity. Beyond it begins that development of human power, which is its own end, the true realm of freedom, which, however, can flourish only upon that realm of necessity as its basis. The shortening of the working day is its fundamental premise." [3]

But this is only one, and by no means the most important meaning which the term "materialism" has in Marxist doctrine. Rather, it is used in a number of different senses, and Engels himself poked fun at those who cling to the view that materialism means "gluttony and guzzling, peep shows and joys of the flesh, arrogance, greed, miserliness, avarice, profit-making, and stock exchange swindles." [4]

We shall see in a later chapter that Marxism uses the term "materialism" to denote what philosophers customarily call "realism," that is, the assertion that the world around us is in existence independently of our senses. We shall not examine this statement any further at this point. What it means and why it is important for Marxist theory will be discussed in Chapter 3. Here, instead, we wish to ask ourselves, why the Marxists insist on calling what philosophy terms "realism," "materialism."

The reason is that a second dogma is contained in their materialist position: not only do they assert that an outside world exists objectively, but they also claim that we can say something about the substance of this real world; and this substance is *matter*. Realism in itself would be perfectly compatible with a view which holds that the objectively existing world is made up, say, of spirit, or mind, or some other nonmaterial element. But according to Marxism, reality is material. Everything that exists can be reduced to matter; all events can be reduced to material processes. If there is mind or spirit, if there are traditions and beliefs and psychological processes, these are either products, or derivatives, of matter, or else they are themselves considered to be a part of matter.

In taking this materialist stand, as historians and social scientists, Marx and Engels sought to repudiate the view of history taken by the German philosopher, Hegel, whose work so much influenced their writings both positively and negatively. Hegel, too, had been a realist in that he attributed objective existence to the world, independent of our senses. But the substance of history, in his eyes, was essentially spiritual: historical evolution was the process by which reason was unfolding and fulfilling itself. All events and institutions were but manifestations of this rational idea; to use a Marxian term, they should be seen as the institutional superstructure built by the idea itself. Marx asserted that this relationship between ideas and institutions must be reversed. *History is not the unfolding of ideas, but of social institutions and social relationships.* A given society is not characterized by its spirit (which becomes incarnate in institutions), but by its social relationships, of which the society's ethos, the spirit of its way of life, is only a surface manifestation.

The essential "spiritualism" of Hegel's philosophy of history did not prevent him from being a keen sociologist whose research on the social structure of his age was to have a profound influence on German social science. Nor did the materialism of Marx's view of history lessen the interest which he, in his turn, showed in ideas. Hence it might seem that his disagreement with Hegel was idle splitting of hairs over what came first, the chicken or the egg. But this is not correct. Implicit in the Marxist materialist view of history is a definite stand on an important problem of social science. This problem concerns the role of ideas in social change. In the name of materialism Marx and Engels broadly criticized the widespread notion that ideas could wreak substantial changes in the world. "Ideas," wrote Marx, "can never lead beyond an old state of the world, but only beyond the ideas of the old state of the world. As a matter of fact, ideas cannot lead to a thing. It requires men employing practical force to carry out ideas." [5] Changing one's ideas, Marx and Engels asserted, leads only to passivity and amounts to no more than demanding that the things which exist be given a different interpretation. But that is the same as recognizing the existing state — by means of a different interpretation. Those who do not grasp this, they say, only deceive themselves. "We know very well what it means to 'step out of everything that exists.' It is the old fancy notion that the state will collapse automatically as soon as all members step out of it and that money loses its value if all workers refuse to accept it. Alone the hypothetical form of this sentence expresses the fantastic character and impotency of the pious wish . . ." [6]

The term "ideas" as used in this context must be understood in a very broad sense, to include will and attitudes, in short, everything that has to do with the human mind. But, if ideas, in this sense of the word, are mere derivations of something else, is not this a denial of free will? Does it not reduce man to a puppet of history, who may indeed assert his will, who may even codify his will or that of the community in laws and statutes, but who will, nonetheless, act as the structure of his society compels him to act? This is indeed what Marxism seems to assert. Listen to the words of Marx, taken from his defense speech before the Cologne jury which acquitted him in 1849:

> Society does not rest upon law This is a juridical fiction. Just the reverse is the truth. Law rests on society, it must be the expression of the general interest that springs from the material production of a given society against the arbitrariness of any single individual.
> Here, the code of laws which I hold in my hands has not created modern civil society. It happened just the other way. The civil society that arose in the eighteenth and developed in the nineteenth century found its legal expression in the code. As soon as it ceases to correspond with the social conditions, the code will be as effete as waste paper.

Or hear this much clearer expression, written by Marx a few years later:

> . . . men make their own history . . . not just as they please; they do not make it under circumstances chosen by themselves, but under circumstances directly found, given, and transmitted from the past.[7]

In short, the actions of men are not freely willed, according to Marx and Engels, but are, instead, determined by the environment.[8]

Nonetheless, Marx and Engels attached tremendous importance to ideas and to will as levers of social change. Keen students of the French Revolution, they explained its course by the ideas of its leaders. Robespierre and Saint-Just, they held, wanted to establish an ideal political community on the model of an idealized Athenian or Roman republic. They wanted to implant republican virtues in the people of France, by force of the Terror, if necessary; and although they failed in this, they did perform a service to the progress of mankind by smashing the remnants of the aristocratic state and clearing the way for a free flourishing of bourgeois relationships. Napoleon's intentions were similarly summed up by Marx and Engels. To them, he represents the last attempt to revive the Terror, the last attempt to establish the state for its own sake, against the power of the propertied class, which Napoleon recognized, but sought to exploit for his political purposes.[9]

By pointing out that the Jacobins and Napoleon fell under the pressure of the rising bourgeoisie, Marx and Engels *reassert the ultimate determinacy of economic relationships.* To us, at this point, it is more important to realize that they recognize the importance of ideas and political action as factors which shape historical events. Yet this is in no way incompatible with the "determinism" of their view. What they say is not that ideas, mind, will, or intentions are ineffective. All that is denied is the effectiveness, or even the existence, of any "free will." To maintain the correctness of their theory, Marx and Engels need only show that the "false" ideology of Napoleon and the Jacobins was itself determined by the manner in which the bourgeoisie grew to supremacy within the womb of the *ancien régime* and its social relationships.

History, in the eyes of Marx and Engels, is not something that men suffer; it is something they make;[10] and in the making of history, ideas, too, may play their role; for, as Engels put it, they are "part of the material world." [11] History, for them, is the result of forces, among which are man's ideas, ideals, and imagination, his will and his intentions. But they held that man is as much an object as he is the subject of history, and they set themselves the task not only of determining precisely when and where and to what degree man is either subject or object, but also of liberating mankind from the external forces which still hold him in subjection. By uncovering the forces determining human conduct, they sought to make man, the object, conscious of his subjugation to historical circumstances, so that he might emancipate himself and become the sovereign maker of history.

Meanwhile, man might act under the compulsion of historical conditions, but history was still the product of man's actions and of man's actions only. If history is, to them, not the product of ideas, that does not mean it is the product of external material forces. Instead, it is the result of man's revolutionary action: "Not criticism, but revolution, is the driving force of history and also of religion, philosophy, and other theories." [12] Or, as Marx wrote shortly after the completion of the *German Ideology:*

The materialist doctrine that man is the product of circumstances and education, hence that a changed man is the product of different circumstances and changed education, forgets that circumstances are changed by that very man and that the educator himself has to be educated.

The coincidence of change of circumstances with [change of] human activity can be grasped and rationally understood only as revolutionary change by human action.[13]

We can now summarize what has been said about the meaning of materialism for Marx. First, we have seen that it implies an awareness of man's material problems of wrestling with the forces of nature. Second, we remarked, in passing, that it is a metaphysical statement concerning the material reality of man's environment, a statement customarily characterized as philosophical realism. Finally, it was shown that it implies a theory concerning the influence of man's will and intentions, his opinions and ideas, on the course of history. Here we saw that Marx cannot be classified either as a determinist or as an opponent of determinism. In his opinion, history is the product of human action, even while men are products of history. Historical conditions determine the way man makes subsequent history, but these historical conditions are themselves the result of human action. The individuals, groups, or classes, of a given period are cast into a situation which they themselves have not made. It has, indeed, been made by their ancestors; so that man, being a product of history, is the product of his ancestors' actions. The basic point of departure is never history, but man, his situation, his problems, and his responses.

The much-belabored dilemma of free will versus determinism is thus no problem for Marxism. This is one of the essentially modern features of Marxist sociology. And that it is a sociology must be emphasized.[14] Much as Marxist scholars, from Engels down to contemporary Communists, have attempted to write Marxist natural science, the original writings of Marx and Engels in which their whole ideology is laid out deal exclusively with the development of social institutions and social relationships. Whenever Nature is mentioned in these basic writings, it is treated as nothing else than one factor in the development of society. The hero and the center of the story is always man.

Marx and Engels, as we have already pointed out, intended to engage in the scientific investigation of man's institutions and their history. Thus aiming to be scientists, they announced that they wanted to eliminate philosophy, that is, a speculative system independent of social science from such an investigation. "When you begin to describe reality," they wrote, "then an independent philosophy loses its existence-medium. In its place may be found, at the most, a summary of the general results abstracted from an investigation of the historical development of man . . ."[15] In common-sense language, this amounts to a demand that social science let the facts speak for themselves as much as possible, and that it should go "from things to concepts, not from concepts to things," as one Soviet writer put it.[16] "In all fields," Engels wrote, "the task is no longer to invent inter-relations in our heads, but to detect them in facts . . ."[17]

The Economic Theory of History

"The task is to detect inter-relations . . ." Indeed, Marxism is one mighty effort to make valid generalizations concerning the way in which the multiple forces at play in human society are interrelated, and how they affect each other. It is an attempt to draw a vast and complex blueprint of our entire social structure, in its social, economic, political, historical and psychological dimensions. In order to accomplish this task of making a systematic study of human society, it has developed a conceptual scheme concerning the integration of these multiple forces and the manner in which they react on each other. This working hypothesis as developed by Marx and Engels is commonly known as *historical materialism*.

The adoption of a broad conceptual framework is a device used by almost all social scientists. It is an attempt to see facts in a certain order or arrangement, to see them in a functioning totality in which everything fits together. One step removed from the purely empirical observation of facts, this device is also removed from unchallengeable scientific reliability. For, going beyond mere observation, it imputes a very specific relationship to the facts observed.

In order to understand this procedure, we may compare the social scientist with the hero of our popular detective stories. Like the social scientist, the detective trying to solve a crime starts with a number of facts. Or, it would be more accurate to say that a number of facts startle him: the discovery that a crime has been committed startles the hero of detective fiction to undertake the job of finding out more facts, indeed as many facts as possible, so that the criminal can be found and convicted.

The number of data that might possibly be relevant to the case on hand, however, may be extremely great. All possible details about the lives and contacts of the people already involved in the case, and about their physical environment, must be gathered, and every new detail may open up a complexity of new leads. How can this enormous collection of data be handled? How can the amount of facts that must be collected be cut down?

In order to do this, the hero of detective fiction takes off in another direction: in addition to gathering facts, he *makes up a fictitious story* which is designed so as to accommodate all the facts he already has in a *plausible explanation*. He may call this story a *theory*, or a *hypothesis*. The requirement that his theory must be plausible is important. It has the effect of limiting his imagination in inventing his theory. In other words, even though a theory is fiction as long as it has not been completely verified (that is, until the case has been solved), it should not be fantastic fiction. It should be based on previously observed facts, on accepted generalizations about human behavior, and equally accepted generalizations about the customs and mores of the culture or subculture in which the act being investigated may have been committed. Thus, the detective investigating the disappearance of a person from an American city in 1953 would hardly suppose that cannibals might have eaten him. A sensible detective would also exclude supernatural agents like demons, gods, or Reason Unfolding Itself from his theory.

The benefits of making up a plausible theory about a case under investigation are obvious: such a theory helps the detective be suggesting what would and what would not be relevant to further investigation, what leads should fruitfully be followed, and what might safely be abandoned. These benefits will accrue even though it is usually found that more than one theory has been made up out of the knowledge already available. The known facts, in other words, lend themselves to different, and conflicting, interpretations. In some cases, the hero of the detective story will make up alternative theories himself; more often, we find his hypothesis pitted against those of his various collaborators and competitors. His wife, the rookie cop, or the lieutenant from the homicide squad — they all make up different theories and, consequently, follow different leads in their investigations.

The chief difference between the work of the detective and that of the social scientist — apart from the limited objective of the former's quest for knowledge — is the fact that crimes are solved, at least in the detective story, while the theories of social scientists remain forever pitted against each other, for lack of definitive verification. Yet, even though there is never a final solution in social science, some theories are certainly much more plausible than others. The theoreticians of social science are constantly at work defining the standards to be adopted in making up hypotheses, and one can apply such standards even though they may not be recognized as valid by all. In claiming scientific validity for their theories, Marx and Engels really meant to say that their hypotheses were in fact the first completely plausible explanation of history. Let us now see what story they invented in this attempt to make sense out of the available historical data.

The interpretation Marx and Engels imposed on their sociology is said to be an *economic* interpretation. Let us first hear Marx give an exposition of this, and then examine the justification (plausibility) and the implications of this economic theory of history.

When the various elements that make up this theory are pieced together from the writings of Marx and Engels, it becomes apparent that, as in most traditional sociological systems, a concept of *human nature* serves as point of departure. True enough, they used to scoff at abstract theories of human nature, asserting that human nature changes with its environment, and that man must be seen, not divorced from, but within the context of his culture, a view which modern social science tends to share. Although Marx and Engels maintained that the *premise* of their sociology was *man*, they were careful to add that they did not have in mind any absolute definition, but man as a concrete historical phenomenon, man as a member of a given culture.[18] And they sought to demonstrate that all the bourgeois theories which did use the concept of human nature were, in fact, abstracting their image of man from the actual living man of capitalist conditions.

Modern social science, without raising the fuss which Marx and Engels made over the concept of human nature, has come to regard it as outmoded. Marx and Engels, however, in spite of their antagonism to it, have nevertheless held a very abstract conception of man, divorced from historical particularities and cultural conditioning, an essential premise of all their theories. This is Engels' concept of man as a "conscious and purposive animal,"[19] which is, at first sight, a purely rationalistic model of man.[20] We shall see later that "consciousness and purposiveness," that is, rationality, the capacity to recognize his real interests and to fight for them intelligently, are the indispensable presuppositions of the whole mechanism of class relations. At the same time, we shall see that Marxism simultaneously contains an elaborate theory of man's irrationality which is, amazingly, derived from the very rational model of man that is assumed in the beginning.

Consciousness could here be defined as man's awareness of himself and his environment, or, better, of himself within his environment. An essential element of this consciousness is the awareness that the environment is, or can be, hostile to the preservation of man's life. This leads directly to purposiveness, which we might define as the plans of man to master his environment and turn it from a hostile into a useful force. Marxism refers to the application of consciousness and purpose (intelligence) as *labor*. The purpose of labor is to obtain from the environment the means to preserve the life of the individual and the species; hence the entire struggle of man with his environment is a struggle for the appropriation of nature, and this appropriation of nature is what Marxism calls *production*.[21] Given the definitions on which the concept of production is based, it is clear that in man only is life a *conscious* struggle with the environment; hence only human life takes the form of production, so that Marx and Engels could write: "Man differs from the animal in that he *produces*."[22]

Obviously, the concept of production is here used in the broadest possible sense of acquiring mastery over one's environment. Used in this sense, the statement that man differs from the animal in that he produces is indeed correct but also rather banal. Clearly, animals are not equipped to do more than to *adjust* to their environment, whereas man has potentialities of creating the most far-reaching changes in his environment, to suit his own purposes.

To refer to this view of man the producer as an economic view is somewhat misleading. Still, the economic interpretation means, at first, no more than this: in trying to explain the history of man and his institutions, the essential thing to look for is the manner in which men have gone about the task of mastering their environment.

On the other hand, Marxist usage does restrict the meaning of the term "production." The individual's environment is not only nature, but also his society; and Marx stresses this whenever he speaks of man's consciousness. As a matter of fact, the word "consciousness" is customarily used by him to mean a consciousness of the self within the social environment, that is, social consciousness. Production, however, means almost exclusively the mastery of the natural environment: "All production is the appropriation of nature by the individual within and through a certain form of society." [23] Hence the definition of man as an animal which produces implies that the struggle with the natural environment is the basic activity of man, of which the struggle with the social environment is only a derivative, a by-product. This view of man's social conflicts as a by-product of his struggle against nature is one of the essential elements of Marxism. It is this view which characterizes Marxism as an economic interpretation of history. At the same time it must be realized that we have understood nothing about Marxist theory if we are satisfied with thus characterizing it.

Note the last words in the sentence quoted above. They are the key to Marxist social theory. First of all, the sentence implies that production is always a social, not an individual, activity: "Production by isolated individuals outside society . . . is as great an absurdity as the idea of the development of language without individuals living and talking to one another." [24] Second, and more important, Marx here implies that there may be different *forms of society*, in and through which individuals engage in the production of the necessities of life. Now, the task which Marx and Engels, as social scientists, imposed on themselves was nothing else than to study the various forms of society, the varous types of social organization that have been developed in man's attempt to master his natural environment, and to trace the development of mankind from one form of society to another.

If a form of society is seen primarily as a way of organizing production, as Marxism does see it, at least one of its key features must be the *division of labor*. This is indeed the contention of Marxist theory. But the division of labor, in turn, is intimately linked with a culture's technological attainments; there can be no blacksmiths in a society which has not learned how to smelt iron ore. Now, Marxism regards the *class structure* of a society as a broader form of the division of labor; hence the class structure, too, is linked with technological development.

For instance, Marxism cannot conceive that the machine age could have come about without the existence of free labor, nor of a proletariat without machines. At a certain time in history, a certain class structure and a certain stage of technological development presuppose each other, and neither force nor law can for long periods maintain social relationships that do not correspond to the mode of production. Laws, Marx admits, "can freeze certain property relations"; for instance, they can maintain large-scale land ownership. But, he continues, "such laws have economic validity only when large-scale property of land is in harmony with the social production, as for instance in England." Conversely, a premature breakup of feudal property, like the parcellization of land after the French Revolution, will not be able to maintain itself: "In spite of these laws, real property consolidated again." [25]

Similarly, Engels, in his comparative study of "gentile" societies in North America, Greece, Rome, Ireland, Scotland, Russia, and Germany, tried to show that like modes of production make for like societies. Comparing the social relations prevailing in the late Roman Empire with those characterizing the Carolingian state, four centuries later, he found striking similarities. These similarities, he wrote, "proved only two things: first, that the social structure and the property relations in the declining Roman Empire corresponded perfectly to the then level of production in agriculture and industry, and had thus been inescapable; and, second, that this level of production had neither sunk considerably nor risen considerably during the following four hundred years, that therefore they had again produced the same property distribution and the same classes of population with the same necessity." [26]

This intimate interdependence of tools with social organization, which Marxist theory stresses, makes it difficult to define a certain key term in Marxist sociology. This term is *the forces of production*.[27] It is of the most crucial importance because these forces of production are regarded as the basic feature on the state of which the entire social structure depends. "Assume a particular state of development in the *productive forces* of man," writes Marx, "and you will get a particular form of commerce and consumption. Assume particular stages of development in *production, commerce, and consumption,* and you will have a corresponding social structure, a corresponding organization of the family, of orders or of classes, in a word, a corresponding civil society. Presuppose a particular *civil society,* and you will get particular political conditions, which are only the official expression of civil society." [28]

Marx thus presents a theory of interrelations in which one set of facts is made dependent on, or determined by, certain other, and hence more basic, facts. And he seems to distinguish four distinct levels or layers of basis and superstructure, of which the lower layer is seen as the precondition of the higher one, as follows:

4. particular political conditions
3. the social structure, or civil society
2. the prevailing mode of production, commerce, and consumption
1. the state of development in the productive forces

It seems from this quotation that the material forces of production, that is, the tools and skills that have been acquired, are thought to be the principal determinant from which all other social phenomena derive. Technology would be the determining force in history; the Marxist theory would have to be interpreted as *technological determinism*. Many students of Marx, both followers and critics, have indeed taken this view, which Hallowell expresses very well by writing that "history, for Marx, is intelligible because it is a history of technology; tools are man-made, and what is man-made is intelligible." [29]

It is nevertheless necessary to reject this interpretation. In spite of Marx's statement quoted above, the term "forces of production" in most of his writings must have had either a much broader meaning, or (if it really meant nothing else than technology), something more than this was considered by him to be the element which determines all other features of society. Anyone who has familiarized himself with a good deal of the writings of Marx and Engels will recognize that the crucial feature around which their whole theory is constructed is the *class structure* of a given society, not its technology.

In his critical review of Proudhon's *La philosophie de la misère*, Marx drew a biting parody of the way in which the German idealist school, and Proudhon as its imitator, allegedly were writing history. "Let us grant with M. Proudhon," he writes, "that real history . . . is the historical sequence in which ideas, categories, and principles have manifested themselves. Each principle has had its own century in which to manifest itself. The principle of authority, for example, had the eleventh century, just as the principle of individualism had the eighteenth century. In logical sequence, it was the century that belonged to the principle, and not the principle that belonged to the century. In other words, it was the principle that made the history, and not the history that made the principle." [30]

It is against this parody that Marx presents his own interpretation, as follows: "When . . . we ask ourselves why a particular principle was manifested in the eleventh or in the eighteenth century rather than in any other, we are necessarily forced to examine minutely what men were like in the eleventh century, what they were like in the eighteenth, what were their respective needs, their productive forces, their mode of production, the raw materials of their production — in short what were the relations between man and man which resulted from all these conditions of existence." [31] We see in this passage that the "relations between man and man" are indeed conceived of as the "result" of all the various material conditions of existence; in that sense we might regard Marxist theory as some sort of technological determinism. It is equally clear, however, that this relationship between technology and the social structure is of little interest to Marx. Instead, he takes the economic structure of society as the basis from which to begin all further investigations of history and society. The economic structure may be determined; but its importance for Marxist theory lies in the fact that it, in turn, determines. There is a famous statement by Marx which sums up this essential core of the economic interpretation:

> In the social production which men carry on they enter into definite relations that are indispensable and independent of their will; these relations of production correspond to a definite stage of development of their material forces of production. The sum total of *these relations of production constitutes the economic structure* of society — the real foundation on which rise legal and political superstructure and to which definite forms of social consciousness correspond.[32]

Moreover, the term "relations of production" is, in Marxian usage, but a synonym of the term "class structure." The class structure therefore is the key feature of any society which a Marxist investigates before searching for any other data.[33] Of technology, Marx speaks only as an important key to the understanding of this basic structure of society.[34]

There are two ways in which Marxism implicitly defines classes. First of all, they are defined by the *function* they fulfill in the society's process of production, and not primarily by the distribution of income and other benefits. Inequalities of distribution and opportunities, though assumed to be part of every division of society into different classes, are seen more as a by-product of the social division of labor, not as its chief distinguishing characteristic. Yet, the very existence of inequalities leads to the second method of defining classes which Marxism uses.

Marxism asserts that all relationships between classes are necessarily exploitative relationship; there are always some classes who carry the main burden of labor while enjoying the smallest share of the social product, while other classes live in comparative leisure and reap the greatest material benefits. What, asks Marx, enables the exploiter class to maintain its position of dominance, and to perpetuate exploitative relationships? The answer is *power*. But what is the source of this power? It cannot be greater numbers; for customarily the exploiter class is numerically inferior to the laboring classes. It is not the possession of the means of warfare and suppression; this too is considered rather a by-product of the ruling class's dominant position. The basis on which the power of the ruling classes rests in the Marxian view, is *the control it wields over the essential means of production and communication*. It is this control which enables a class to exploit all those classes which do not have such control, to maintain economic, social, and political inequalities. It is this control which makes a class into the *ruling class*.[35]

In studying a society, the first step in the Marxist procedure, then, would be to determine the technological mode of production, who controls this at all levels, and what classes are without any control at all. In other words, how are the essential means of production and communication distributed, and how is the production process organized in accordance with this distribution? What is the class structure of the society under investigation, and what is the role of the different classes in the process of production? The next step would be to take an over-all cultural survey of the society — its political and legal systems; its social institutions, customs, mores, and traditions; and the hopes, aspirations, fears, and anxieties of its members. What scientific systems have its members developed, what social theories, what religion or philosophy? And how are all these features of the culture (or *superstructure*) related to the class structure, which is considered the *base* of the society as a whole? For, that they are intimately related to it is taken for granted by the theory of Marx and Engels, even though they themselves occasionally warned that the theory should not be applied uncritically and rigidly.[36] We must add, however, that neither they nor their followers paid sufficient heed to this warning.

Anyone who is familiar with the writings of Marx and Engels

must be aware of their sharply polemical tone. The two men were constantly battling and fulminating against what they correctly regarded as inadequate approaches to an understanding of history and society. They obviously rejected the "kings-and-battles" approach to history which is still today so prevalent in the textbooks which we hand our school children. They equally opposed that "ideological determinism" according to which ideas are carried to their logical conclusion in the historical process. Most important, however, they fought against the mechanistic-metaphysical method of liberal social theory, the method in which a theory of human relationships is deduced, rationally, from a strict definition of human nature. Liberal theory develops its entire conception of social organization from the axiom that all individuals, considered equal to one another, rationally pursue the maximization of their pleasure and the minimization of their pain.

Contrary to widespread belief, Marxism does not substitute an environmental approach, an institutional determinism for these theories. It demands, rather, that the social scientist must seek out the human relationships to be found in the division of labor in the production process, as the key to an understanding of the society. It believes that these human relationships express themselves in every *institution*, every *idea*, and every *thing* produced by mankind. Political and legal institutions evolve as the forms in which the class structure molds itself. Ideas are regarded as reflections of the existing social order, its problems, tensions, habits, and traditions. Even a commodity is, to Marx, chiefly the product of human labor; commodity exchange, nothing else than an involved transaction between a number of human beings who produce. People, not things, enter into a relationship in the market — another instance of the attack against liberal theory. "The subject matter of economics is not things," wrote Engels, "but relations between persons and, in the last instance, between classes; these relations, however, are always tied to things and take on the appearance of things." [37]

The economist who regards the market as a place where commodities are related to one another by means of prices is, according to Marxism, indulging in *commodity fetishism*. In Marxist terminology, the concept of fetishism is used to denote the practice of endowing man-made institutions with unchangeable laws of their own, abstracting them from their historical, human determinateness. "There is," wrote Marx, "a definite social relation between men, that assumes, in their eyes, the fantastic form of a relation between things. . . . [In the realm of religion] the productions of the human brain appear as independent beings endowed with life, and entering into relation both with one another and the human race. So it is in the word of commodities with the products of men's hands. This I call the Fetishism which attaches itself to the products of labor, as soon as they are produced as commodities." [38] A key concept in Marx's theory of ideology, this is his methodological explanation of the fact that, in his opinion, all human consciousness has, heretofore, been false consciousness. This is a topic which will be dealt with in a subsequent chapter.

The approach outlined above is one with which modern sociologists and anthropologists have little to quarrel. This applies particularly to cultural anthropology, which developed entirely independently from Marxism.[39] It is only the economic interpretation, according to which the division of labor is the essence of the social structure, and the production of the means of subsistence, the most essential activity of man, which has remained highly controversial. Hardly a social scientist would underestimate the contributions to the understanding of society which were made on the basis of this interpretation. But it might still be worthwhile to speculate why Marxism rejects all attempts to use something other than economic pursuits, and the social relations of economic pursuits, as the basic structure of society, the central variable to which all other variables are functionally related. The reason seems to lie in the fact that Marxism is so intensely preoccupied with social change; and in comparison with the mode of production, other aspects of human culture are relatively constant, and static. We can probably say that kinship structure, national traditions, culture patterns, and basic human drives have time to exert their deepest influence on the entire social structure only in periods or cultures where economic development is slow or nonexistent. Conversely, periods of rapid change and revolutionary transition are characterized both by the disintegration or corrosion of well-established cultural institutions and behavior patterns and by the prevalence of open class struggle. Since Marx defined classes in economic terms, his preoccupation with times of open class struggle could not but lead to the demand that the social scientist concentrate on economic development,[40] and to the criticism of other orientations as misleading. By this token the Marxist abdicates as a social scientist when he faces the problem of investigating comparatively static periods or cultures. Just as many disciplines of "bourgeois social science" are relatively helpless when they want to investigate periods of crisis, so Marxism is weak in analyzing relatively stable systems.

Given this preoccupation with economic change, the next logical step would be to investigate the precise manner in which the class structure imparts its influence on the culture as a whole and on its different parts. It would be necessary to study the precise nature of the process by which the institutional, emotional, moral, or other superstructure is determined by the economic substructure.

But here Marxism has generally failed. Its followers have traditionally been interested in establishing a close correspondence between superstructure and substructure. Their first attempt in investigating a society is always to match, as it were, these two aspects of the society; and tremendously interesting and suggestive observations have been made in which the development of art, philosophy, and literature, family relations and political institutions, are seen in the light of the changing class structure and the class struggle. The keenest minds among Marxists have developed something like that sixth sense in uncovering correspondences which enables Freudian psychologists to interpret our every thought and act as symbols or expressions of subconscious drives and problems. Lest the impression be created that these words are written with the intention of casting ridicule on the combinations of Marxists or Freudians, it should be pointed out that they are, instead, meant to convey the writer's admiration for the artistic imagination, the brilliance, and the cleverness of those scholars. Even though the correspondences established by them may at times defy the humdrum methods of exact social science — or, perhaps, just because they defy the painstaking efforts of some of the bureaucrats of social science — they are of great value as fresh and exciting ideas. Their suggestive, imagination-stirring quality is ample reason to praise them. And yet, in the cases of both the Freudian and the Marxist, the outsider is often left with a profound feeling of uneasiness because the alleged correspondence which seems so utterly obvious to the devotees has not been explained to his complete satisfaction.

Perhaps the deepest root of our uneasiness may be found in certain methodological difficulties inherent in Marxism. We have learned that Marx and Engels attempted to find a scientific method of enquiry into social processes. This attempt often remained a groping search, particularly since even the best representatives of the Marxist school appear themselves to be somewhat in the dark about the implications of their method.

In particular, Marxism, in a curious way, combines two views of the world which are not easily reconciled, though they may, in the final analysis, be entirely reconcilable. One is a *mechanistic* view of the world; a conception of the universe which regards it as a multitude of things or forces, none of them related or connected in any way, but all of them affecting each other in a clash of matter or energy. The other is a *functional* view of reality as a process of change in a system that is seen in its totality, in which all parts are integrated in the whole and have meaning only within the context of the whole. The outstanding difference between these two views is that the mechanistic one searches into causal chains, because all changes are seen as the effect of some specific action which caused it; whereas the functional view of reality sees all parts of the whole only as *corresponding* to, but not caused by, the other parts and the entire system. The functional system consists of variables that change in step with each other — reciprocally interdependent variables; the mechanistic system consists of constants that enter into one-sided relationships with other individual "atoms," as causes or effects within the totality of parts.

These terms may be extremely bewildering at first, but we shall have occasion to throw some light on them.[41] First, however, it must be pointed out that, purely theoretically, there is no reason why both methods of investigation should not be used by advocates of one and the same theory. On the contrary, an adequate theory of social relationships should certainly integrate these two methods by giving each one its proper place in a broader scheme. It could even be argued that such an integration of the two different methods is precisely what Marx and Engels attempted in their theoretical formulations. If this be true, however, they must be blamed for presenting the problems in terms so bewildering and in a manner so unsystematic, that they themselves could not have been sufficiently aware of the nature of the methodological problem with which they attempted to deal, to have handled it in a manner at all adequate.

Marxist theorists have, in short, not given a clear answer to the question concerning the relationship between mechanistic and nonmechanistic thinking in their method. Since this is to be an exposition of Marxist thought, and not a treatise on the method of social science, it cannot be our task to attempt a solution to this question here. All that needs to be pointed out is that, from all indications, the question has not been answered by Marxism. Consequently, Marxist thinkers have always thought according to both methods, without clearly distinguishing between them, and have therefore managed to confuse themselves and others concerning the nature of their particular approach. Marx slips from one method to another, enjoying the best of both, in an irresponsible fashion. But it is high time that we try to clarify the difference between the mechanistic and the functional method in social science.

The Functional View of Reality

In the third volume of *Capital* Marx made one of his many statements outlining his economic interpretation of history, and began as follows:

The specific economic form, in which unpaid surplus labor is pumped out of the direct producers, determines the relation of rulers and ruled, as it grows immediately out of production itself and reacts upon it as a determining element. Upon this is founded the entire formation of the economic community which grows up out of the

North Carolina Wesleyan College Library

Rocky Mount, North Carolina 27801

conditions of production itself, and this also determines its specific political shape. It is always the direct relation of the owners of the conditions of production to the direct producers, which reveals the innermost secret, the hidden foundation of the entire social construction, and with it of the political form of the relations between sovereignty and dependence, in short, of the corresponding form of the state. The form of this relation between rulers and ruled naturally corresponds always with a definite stage in the development of the methods of labor and of its productive social power.

So far, this sounds familiar. Marx, however, goes on to qualify the statement by acknowledging the influence of noneconomic factors in determining the class structure: "This does not," he wrote, "prevent the same economic basis from showing infinite variations and gradations in its appearance, even though its principal conditions are everywhere the same. This is due to innumerable outside circumstances, natural environment, race peculiarities, outside historical influences, and so forth, all of which must be ascertained by careful analysis." [42]

Obviously, this recognition that the class structure itself is determined by innumerable outside influences does not, in this statement, lessen the cardinal importance of this class structure as the key to the "innermost secret, the hidden foundation of the entire social construction." But a number of times both Marx and Engels made serious qualifications in the theory that the economic substructure inevitably determines the superstructure. Several times they affirmed that elements of the superstructure can acquire independence from the class struggle on the basis of which they arose, that they can stand by themselves and develop in themselves, that they can develop even in contradiction to the ruling order, so that they can serve as the ferment which loosens the hold of the ruling classes over society. Thus Engels wrote to a friend:

According to the materialist conception of history the determining element in history is *ultimately* the production and reproduction in real life. More than this neither Marx nor I have ever asserted. If therefore somebody twists this into the statement that the economic element is the *only* determining one, he transforms it into a meaningless, abstract, and absurd phrase. The economic situation is the basis, but the various elements of the superstructure — political forms of the class struggle and its consequences, constitutions established by the victorious class after a successful battle, etc., forms of law, and then even the reflexes of all these actual struggles in the brains of the combatants: political, legal, philosophical theories, religious ideas and their further development into systems of dogma — these also exercise their influence upon the course of the historical struggles and in many cases preponderate in determining their *forms*. . . .[43]

Here, it seems, we have come to a contradiction in the theories of Marx and Engels. On the one hand, they appear to claim that economic relations are directly determining all historical phenomena. At the same time, however, they water this economic determinism down a good deal when it is criticized as naïve. Yet, do not all the important conclusions of Marxist theory stand or fall with the hypothesis of economic determinism?

The key to the difficulty lies in the meaning of the word "determine" which is customarily used in Marxist theory to describe the relation between the social structure and its superstructure. There are two conflicting interpretations of what this term means. According to one of these interpretations, often referred to as *vulgar Marxism*, the term "determination" is synonymous with the term "cause-and-effect relationship." Hence the statement that the social structure determines the superstructure would mean that the former is the cause, the latter the effect; the superstructure is the direct product, or result, of its base, the social structure. Those who interpret the concept of determination in this manner usually criticize Marxist theory for the narrowness and inadequacy of its economic determinism and argue, with Bernstein, that economics is only one of a number of important factors determining historical processes. The social scientists, Bernstein wrote, must give "full consideration not only to the development and influence of the forces of production and relations of production, but also to the conceptions of law and morals, the historical and religious traditions of an era, the influence of geographical and other natural influences, in which must be included the nature of man himself and his mental capacities." [44]

This criticism is well taken if "determination," as used by Marx and Engels, really does mean "causality," and the qualifications thrown in by Engels, and quoted above, are then indeed in conflict with the theory as originally stated by him and Marx. They would then have to be regarded as a weak and unconvincing afterthought, produced for the sake of saving face. But the interpretation we have so far given the concept of determination is not the only possible one. The term is, in fact, quite ambiguous and may be misleading. And the very fact that such a vague term was used by Marx and Engels indicates that they themselves were not at all clear what its connotation was meant to be. As we shall see shortly, there is a good deal of reason to suppose that it did not signify a cause-and-effect relationship so much as, rather, a functional relationship. We may find that Marx and Engels were not primarily interested in what had been the cause of what; instead, their aim was, probably, to demonstrate how all phenomena were integrated and interrelated as a total system, how this system as a whole worked, and what its pattern of development might be.

For Marxism views society as a social universe, an all-embracing system in which everything is related to everything else.[45] Let us assume, for the moment, that this interrelation of everything was meant by them to be a cause-and-effect relation. In this case, we should have to conclude that, far from imposing any sort of economic monism, Marx and Engels took as their point of departure a causal pluralism in which everything could be traced to a virtually infinite multiplicity of effective causes. Clearly, such a view leads to an impasse. Those who subscribe to the vulgar-Marxist position maintain that the way out of this impasse was to state categorically that economic causes were always, or most of the time, more important than others, an arbitrary decision which social scientists are unlikely to accept. Hence, the empiricism of Marx's critics who demand that the social scientist find out, in every individual instance, what the chain of causes has been.

But Marx and Engels have denounced this empirical approach as shallow eclecticism. There might be some good sense in this attitude, if indeed they substituted functional thinking for the cause-and-effect thinking of both empiricists and vulgar Marxists. Negatively stated, this would mean that cause-and-effect thinking is abandoned as a futile undertaking, given the infinite multiplicity of causes and effects that can be linked with any individual thing or event.

Function is a concept denoting mutual dependence of two or more variables. In functional relationships, a change in any one variable conditions a change in the other variable(s). It is not always possible to determine unambiguously what changes will occur when one variable is changed. In mathematics, the unknown variable x may turn out to have both a positive and a negative sign; in history, a crucial change may, quite similarly, bring with it contradictory phenomena. The functional view thus appears to be consonant with the dialectical approach, with which we shall have to deal before long.[46]

Functional thinking implies a view of a total system endowed with a *function*, or, as Talcott Parsons put it,

the conception of the empirical system as a "going concern." It is . . . the functional reference of all particular conditions and processes *to the state of the total system as a going concern* which provides the logical equivalent of simultaneous equations in a fully developed system of analytical theory. This appears to be the only way in which dynamic *interdependence* of variable factors in a system can be explicitly analyzed without the technical tools of mathematics and the operational and empirical prerequisites of their employment.[47]

We know already what the "total system as a going concern" of Marxist theory is: it is the society geared for production and organized in classes, which are dependent on each other even while they struggle against each other. Everything is functionally related to this struggle of the classes, so that the class struggle, and the entire class structure in which the conflict is raging, becomes the central coefficient, as it were, in the total system and its development. Analyze it, Marx claims, and you will have, not the most important factor in the development of society, but the determining essence of that society.[48]

In the writings of Marx and Engels, the functional approach is hidden behind ambiguous words like "conditioning" or "determining"; and yet, a passage like the following shows pretty clearly that Marx thought in functional terms:

. . . production, distribution, exchange, consumption, *are not identical*, but . . . they all form members of a totality, differences within unity. . . . A certain [form of] production thus determines certain [forms of] consumption, distribution, exchange, and *certain relations of these different factors to each other*. Yet production, too, *in its onesided form*, is in turn determined by other factors.[49]

Again, this view is little concerned with cause-and-effect relationships, just as the interdependent variables of mathematical functions are not related to each other as causes and effects. Take any phenomenon, watch it being analyzed by Marxist sociology, and you will find this statement confirmed, in the main. Whether he considers political institutions, laws, social customs or ideologies, Marx is not satisfied with an attempt to explain their causal origins. As a matter of fact, such attempts are often unsuccessful. He will, in addition, attempt to explain what a given institution, idea, or tradition does, whom it harms and whom it benefits — in short, what function it fulfils in the operation of the social system and in the class struggle. Once questions of this sort are asked, the mere existence of the phenomenon is virtually taken for granted. Everything that exists must appear as an accident, once causality, because it has become unwieldy or uninteresting, is dropped from consideration. In fact, a number of Marxists have come out with the assertion that, viewed from the point of view of its causal origin, everything is accidental. In his curious Hegelian jargon, Engels wrote that "accident is the form in which necessity exists." "Necessity" in this context can, of course, only mean a functional or teleological necessity, not a cause-and-effect determination. What matters is not the origins of phenomena but their functional relationship to the class struggle. Here some things are of central significance whereas others are more incidental. But whether they are central or incidental, all are considered to be accidental as far as their causal origin is concerned.[50]

What, then, is the meaning of economic determinism in Marxist theory? It means that the total system which Marxism views is human society organized, in a class structure, for the production of life's necessities. All natural and social phenomena that come under observation are seen in functional relationship to this central pursuit and this basic structure of society. This takes on an essentially teleological aspect: it is not arbitrary choice which has made economics the central functional coefficient. Marx and

Engels, as we have seen, assert that economic pursuits are in fact the all-important activity around which all history develops. This means that the economic pursuits of man are seen as the principal conditioning element of historical development, as a framework which limits the range of incidental phenomena that could become socially effective. Since, from the point of view of cause-and-effect analysis, everything is considered accidental, there is, theoretically, no limit to what can arise independently of the economic structure. If, however, accidentally created phenomena are *dysfunctional*, that is, if there is no possible function for them in the social system or in the class struggle going on at a given time, they will not be able to become effective and will therefore wither away, or remain dormant until they have an opportunity to become functional.[51] Thus the economic structure of society cannot prevent dysfunctional features from coming into existence; nor does it make the development of functional features inevitable.[52] What the economic structure does do is predispose a given society for a certain type of superstructure. "This much is clear," wrote Marx, "the Middle Ages could not live on Catholicism, nor the ancient world on politics. It is the manner in which they gained their livelihood which explains, conversely, why politics played the leading role in one, Catholicism in the other society . . . *Already Don Quixote paid for the error of believing that the institution of the knight-errant was compatible with all economic forms of society.*"[53]

Dialectics as the Conceptual Framework of Functional Thought

Our contention that the determinism of Marxist thinking is a functional, not a causal, view of society, is corroborated by the insistence of Marxist scholars on the dialectical approach.

Anyone discussing the meaning of dialectics in the Marxist scheme of concepts is immediately faced with the great difficulty of separating imputed meaning from actual meaning. As we shall try to show, dialectics is said (by Marxists) to be one thing, but, upon examination, will turn out to be something entirely different. The resulting confusion has caused most of those who cling to dialectics to lapse into most unutterable sterility, so that others, accepting the Marxist definition of dialectics at face value, have rejected it with perhaps unwarranted revulsion. We shall find that some of its laws are interesting and suggestive symbols of functional thought.

Following Marx and Engels, who talked in the language of Hegel, contemporary Marxists, proclaiming the virtues of dialectics, will customarily refer to it as a system of logic. The concepts that make up the language of dialectics seem to support this interpretation; for the language of dialectics abounds with the terminology that is familiar to students of logic: we need only think of the concepts "contradiction," "negation," and "identity (or unity) of opposites."

Logic, as defined by most philosophers, is a set of rules by which we control the correctness of our conclusions, that is, of the result of our thinking. In rejecting traditional, or formal, logic, the adherents of dialectics imply that their rules are better. But, when we examine the claims they make for dialectics, we find that their logic is not a better set of rules by which to control the correctness of conclusions. Instead, they praise dialectics over formal logic because it is, they say, a better *reflection of reality*.

Logic, however, is not a reflection of reality, good or otherwise. It is a controlling device to check our method of drawing conclusions, but it says nothing about the content of our thoughts, and does not reveal anything about reality. If, therefore, dialectics is in any way a reflection of reality it differs from, or includes more than, logic. And if Marxists do refer to dialectics as logic, the only explanation is that the word "logic" does not mean for them what it means for other philosophers.

This confusion over the meaning of logic is a hangover from the Hegelian tradition. In Hegel's terminology, logic was not only the rules by which conclusion-making is controlled, but it also expressed the most fundamental law of being, which means that it represented certain knowledge about the real world. Thus Hegelian (and Marxist) logic is not only logic in the strict sense of the word accepted by most contemporary philosophers, but also a kind of ontology, that is, a theory of being, or existence. Now, since Marx and Engels reject the notion of *a priori* knowledge, the most fundamental laws of being must necessarily be empirical, so that logic turns into empirical knowledge.

Thus, dialectics-logic is conceived, first of all, as the rules according to which ideas and concepts are related to each other. But, since thought processes are regarded as reflections of material processes, the logic of thought must correspond to the logic of facts and events. And, vice versa, the ontology of actual processes is applied to ideas and becomes an ontology of thought — called "logic." [54]

Marxist dialectics can therefore be defined, *by us*, as the most abstract description of how phenomena in the real world are related to each other. And the first statement made by dialectics is a negative one: Phenomena are not related to each other in a cause-and-effect relationship. Using a somewhat different terminology, the adherents of dialectics assert that phenomena are not related to each other in a mechanistic way. Dialectical materialism proclaims its opposition to mechanistic materialism, which views reality as a system of energy-matter in which all processes occur strictly in accordance with the laws of cause and effect. Such strict causal thinking is rejected by the dialecticians. They point out, instead, that most cause-and-effect relationships are at least reciprocal: in affecting and changing other variables, any given variable must also change itself because the change in its environment makes itself felt. As the dialecticians put it, *everything is at once cause and effect of the development in which it partakes*. But this is merely an odd and clumsy way of describing a functional relationship.

In criticizing the mechanistic conception of change or process, Marxists are likely to dismiss it as a *metaphysical* view. This epithet is used by them in a very special Hegelian meaning, to denote an atomistic and pluralistic approach to reality, an approach which neglects the reciprocity of total interrelation. "Metaphysical" is, to the Marxist, the opposite of "dialectical." "To the metaphysician, things and their mental reflexes — ideas — are isolated, are to be considered one after the other and apart from each other, are objects of investigation fixed, rigid, given once and for all time. He thinks in absolutely irreconcilable antitheses." [55]

This critique, by Engels, of metaphysics contains an implicit affirmation of the functional view. And we can single out three different elements of this view which are, by implication, endorsed in the statement. First of all, by criticizing the metaphysicians for viewing things as isolated, Engels demands that they be seen in integration, as elements of a *total system*. Second, by refusing to regard objects of investigation as fixed and rigid, he comes out in favor of treating all objects as *variables*. Finally, he implies that only this view makes *reconcilable contradictions* out of irreconcilable antitheses. Having dwelled at length on the first of these points, we shall have to discuss the other two in a little more detail.

Marxism criticizes traditional (Aristotelian) metaphysics for conceiving of things too statically. Nothing that exists, it implies, ever remains the same. All things are in constant flux and change. This position is as old as Heraclitus, who observed that "we never step into the same river twice." What Heraclitus said about the river, Marxism says about social institutions and human beings themselves, revealing thereby its preoccupation with social processes and social change, its insistence on historical perspective in social science. This attitude, as such, is sensible enough. But the philosophical expression it has been given in the writings of Engels is highly inadequate and misleading. In one of his favorite examples, he speaks of motion, and observes that a thing which is in motion is at any given moment at a certain point within the line of movement, but at the same time it is not at that point, as it is moving away from it. Similarly, anything that is changing is simultaneously itself and not not itself any more. A is not only A, it is also Not-A. We see here the Aristotelian logic of identity completely dissolved and repudiated, on the grounds that, according to empirical observation, all things are in flux.

Now, first, empirical observation does not in any way tell us that all things are constantly changing. H_2O will always be water, even though it may be in a solid, liquid, or gaseous state, depending on the temperature and pressure prevailing at the moment. Only if it is subjected to chemical change will we have something other than water. But then we can no longer speak about H_2O. It is not correct to say, in this instance, that A is both A and

Not-A, or, to "synthesize being and not-being into the concept of becoming" and say that "A becomes Not-A." H_2O is always H_2O and never is in the process of becoming Not-H_2O, at least not until we do away with it altogether by subjecting it to a chemical reaction.

Second, the dissolution of the logic of identity simply means the dissolution of concepts. "A becomes Non-A" really means that "A becomes," or "things change their nature." But when things change their nature, we can no longer speak about them in abstract concepts, but only in combination with adjectival expressions which give them historical *concreteness*. We can no longer generalize about "human nature," but must speak about "human nature under certain conditions." Theories about "the state" must give way to descriptions of "the feudal state," "the imperialist state," or "the political structure of the United States from 1865 to 1890." In short, the opposite of metaphysics, as criticized by Marxism, is not only dialectics but also concreteness; and the two latter terms are often used interchangeably. That is the meaning of the attack Engels made on those who think of objects as "fixed, rigid, given once and for all time."

The criticism of metaphysics as an excessively static view of reality has yet another implication. According to Marx and Engels, matter is not only in constant change, it is also inherently dynamic. The mechanistic conception of reality has also seen all particles of matter as being in constant motion. All change was seen as the effect of the impact which different particles of matter had upon others as they encountered them in their motion. The original source of motion, however, was placed outside the entire system. In contrast, the dialectical view of Marx and Engels places the ultimate source of energy within the system itself and within each particle of matter. In the words of Engels, motion is "inherent in all matter"; all motion is automotion.

A hundred-odd years after Marx and Engels formulated their philosophy, this statement seems extremely crude in its formulation, even though it may be acceptable in what it wants to convey. Indeed, the distinction between matter and energy has become so obscured in modern science that the Marxian assertion seems hopelessly out of date. But in the 'forties of the nineteenth century it had little if any basis in natural science. Instead, Marx and Engels derived it from the historical scheme of Hegel, whose dialectics is a development of ideas, not of matter.

According to Hegelian-Marxist dialectics, the dynamic quality inherent in matter is said to be the result of a certain tension or unbalance within each unit of the material world. Motion and development is seen as the result of a struggle or conflict of opposites contained in unity within each thing. Everything has within itself its own opposite, or everything has within itself struggling opposites, and motion is caused by (or takes the form of) this contradiction.

The concept of the unity and struggle of opposites is a mystifying formula. As many other dialectical terms, the words are borrowed from logic, which gives them a bewildering aspect when dialectics turns from an idealistic to a materialistic image of reality. Moreover, the term "opposite" remains vague and undefined. One glance at the innumerable examples of contradictions mentioned at one time or another by Marxist writers reveals that these terms can be applied or illustrated with the utmost arbitrariness.

And yet, the concept of the unity of opposites is an important symbol for a very specific type of functional relationship. It denotes the reciprocal dependency of conflicting things, a relationship in which two or more things simultaneously presuppose and limit each other. Ambivalent interrelations of this type are almost commonplace to students of modern depth psychology, even though they have not gone through the philosophical school of Hegel. Marx and Engels pointed out that many philosophers of previous ages had thought dialectically without having to formulate any laws of dialectics. Such men as Nicolaus Cusanus and Baruch Spinoza were held up by them as models of dialectical thinking. The terminology of dialectics is therefore no more than a systematization and, supposedly, clarification of scientific methods which have led to brilliant results many times in the past. It is a pity that the actual terms which were adopted by Hegel and his Marxist followers turned out to be so utterly inadequate to this task. Indeed, the terminology of dialectics has much more frequently served to defeat the purpose of systematization and clarification of the functional method.

The curiously ambivalent relationship of reciprocally dependent and conflicting things (usually referred to in Marxism as persons, groups, and classes, but meaning also institutions, processes, and other things) is expressed even more strikingly by some other terms of Hegelian-Marxist dialectics. Opposites that are in unity are said to be negating each other — another term borrowed from logic, which makes no sense unless it is applied only to contradictory ideas. These terms were introduced by Hegel to differentiate his ideas from those of Kant, who had pointed out that there were a number of irreconcilable *antinomies,* each consisting of a pair of statements that were empirically true, but mutually contradictory. According to Kant, the conflict of antinomical statements could not be resolved by empirical investigation. Hegel, in contrast, thought that there were no irreconcilable antinomies, but only reconcilable contradictions, or antitheses. Antithetical ideas, he said, were reconciled by a *synthesis;* the negation would be negated.

The negation of a negation — that means, of course, its reconciliation. The synthesis joins contradictions in a higher unity. Hegel used an ingenious pun to express the ambivalent character of the synthesis. He used the German verb, *aufheben,* to indicate what the synthesis does to the negation, or contradiction. This verb has three distinct meanings: (1) to make void, to eliminate; (2) to lift up; and (3) to preserve. All these meanings are to be conveyed simultaneously when the verb is used with the noun "synthesis," because the negation of the negation supposedly eliminates the contradiction, it lifts the entire problem onto a higher plane, and it preserves the contradictory elements by thus integrating them within a higher unity.

This dialectical *triad* of thesis, antithesis, and synthesis, has usually been understood to signify a developmental scheme, in which the three components of the triad are seen as successive steps in time, antithesis following the thesis, and the synthesis following the antithesis in turn. But the same dialectical terminology has often been used to stand for a functional interrelationship viewed at a particular moment in time. Interpreted in this manner, the antithetical elements are then the parts which compose a whole (the synthesis). Taken by themselves, these parts may be contradictory; they may destroy or limit or exclude each other. But, seen in the broader perspective of the total system, they are functional. This whole is therefore more than its parts, and the parts become reconcilable only in the structured and functional relationship which is the essence of the whole. In the Marxist scheme, the bourgeoisie and the proletariat might be described as antithetical classes; yet their very struggle is seen as the essence of the capitalist system. In Leninist theory, the principles of leadership and democracy may be contradictory, but the principle of *democratic centralism* is supposed to reconcile and unite them in a higher unity. Similarly, Eduard Heimann has observed that freedom and order are antithetical. Driven to their logical conclusion, they exclude each other; and even where both are limited, they also limit each other. But, precisely when both of them are limiting each other, when freedom is fighting order and order is asserting its demands against freedom without either of them swallowing the other, the synthesis of democracy results. Democracy is thus a function of freedom and order.[56]

Opposites may be in functional unity. Conversely, identities may, in a different total context, become contradictory; reconcilables may turn into opposites. The bourgeoisie and the peasantry may be united in struggling against aristocratic privilege. But once their fight is won, their alliance may turn into hostility over the question of how the newly won freedom is to be used and how the free society is to be organized. In the development of an individual's personality, a strong emotional attachment to the parent may turn from a healthy to an unhealthy one when it is carried over beyond a functional intensity or time-span. Marxists would say that, in the above statements, the relationship between bourgeoisie and peasantry, or between child and parent, has been viewed dialectically, that is, within a functional context, within the total structure of the system.

Hence dialectics is meant to serve as a reminder that the total system (always seen as a system undergoing changes) alone gives meaning to its component elements. The mechanistic conception of reality is criticized by the Marxists because it allegedly fails to do this. The mechanistic view, they assert, does indeed see all things as affecting each other; but it also sees everything as a piece of matter-in-motion *within a given universe.* Both the component elements and the universe are given and do not change. In contrast, dialectics is asserted to be a cosmic view, in which the total structure, constantly changing, gives a completely new meaning to the component elements and even creates new things, new relationships, and new institutions. This applies to social institutions, social relationships, ideologies, attitudes, and behavior patterns just as much as it does to artifacts. The general strike, the totalitarian mass party, and the National Labor Relations Board are, all of them, just as much new inventions as the steam engine and pasteurization, or even more so. For technological advances are perhaps built on the basis of the achievements of by-gone centuries of scientific development. Behavior patterns, however, are traced to historical precedents with far greater difficulty. It is highly fallacious to link the oppressive despotism of Russia's tsars directly to the totalitarianism of Soviet rule, or to trace the general strike of the European proletariat to the "strikes" of mediaeval journeymen.[57] In both cases, historians are talking about completely different phenomena, and they would have great difficulty in showing real historical connections between the phenomena they are trying to link up.

Fundamental Questions in Marxist Methodology

The preceding discussion of Marxist dialectics has not exhausted the topic. On the contrary, we shall have to come back to it in later chapters where we shall see that it expresses not only a certain scientific method, but also a political attitude and a profound historical faith. Here our task has been but to adduce and explain those concepts of dialectical terminology which support our contention that Marxism views reality as a functional relationship, and less as a complex of causal chains.

It must be stressed again that the distinction between these two methods is never made explicitly in Marxist writings. We have to interpret it out of their statements and the actual manner of their approach. Moreover, since the terminology of Marxism has been baffling, and the approaches many, it is impossible to take a definite stand concerning the relationship of these two methods in Marxist theory. Mechanistic and antimechanistic ideas are encountered with equal frequency, if not in the writings of Marx himself, then certainly in those of all his followers, including Engels. The change-over from one to the other is at times imperceptible.

On page 30 we pointed out that Marxist theory does not explain the existence of a thing as the last link in a causal chain; instead, it takes its existence for granted as accidental and concentrates on the function which it has in the social system and in the class struggle. This is, however, a one-sided picture. Students of Marxist literature will time and again encounter statements by which the existence of institutions, attitudes, prejudices, and traditions, is explained in terms of cause and effect. Many Marxists tend glibly to explain any attitude of which they do not approve as the direct result of ruling class propaganda, deliberately spread or fostered for the purpose of dividing the proletariat, setting off the lower classes against each other, deflecting the attention of the exploited from the real cause of their misery, or inciting the resentment of the mob which might then be managed for the purposes of the ruling class. Similarly any institution associated with a given social system would be explained as an instrument of coercion, oppression, or manipulation, deliberately created by the ruling classes for the purpose of keeping the lower classes in check.

Now, both ways to deal with the phenomena of political prejudices, traditions, and institutions, are perfectly defensible from the point of view of social science; and it might even be possible to place both methods within the framework of Marxist theory. It is, however, highly doubtful whether Marx and Engels meant to substitute this kind of scapegoat theory for the fetishism of the metaphysical sociologists against whom they fulminated so sharply. Fetishism was the attribution of history-making capabilities to man-made things. The scapegoatism of many Marxists, in turn, is the attribution of historic decision-making to the will, be it free or determined, of classes. It would mean no more than that the heroes of kings-and-battles history books are now replaced by the villains of ruling classes and the heroes of barricade fighters. History is reduced to the actions of the principal antagonists in the struggle of classes; and, as long as the ruling classes dominate this struggle (as they often do according to Marxist theory), history is seen as the artifact of the ruling classes. Even though this view is part of Marxist theory, surely it is not the whole explanation of ideologies which Marxism offers. But if it is the very essence of Marxist theory, then we should have to dismiss this theory as being naïvely rational and mechanistic. To what extent mechanistic thinking is actually a part of the theory conceived by Marx and Engels, therefore, has never been explained satisfactorily.

Another source of uneasiness to the outsider who studies Marxist literature is its pronounced teleological tendency, characterized by the frequent use of words such as "inevitably" — much as some Marxists have tried to explain that word away. Now, teleology is inherent in all functional thinking. After all, the "total system as a going concern" is decidedly a teleological concept; for it implies a direction or an aim toward which the concern is supposed to be going. Teleology, in the sense that an organized end is seen for society, and that this particular organization constitutes the substructure to which all other aspects of that society are functionally related, is scientifically justified, as long as the social scientist remains aware that his particular view is no more than a hypothesis, or, more correctly, an interpretation. The difference between hypotheses and interpretations is crucial for an understanding of the functional method. Hypotheses are subject to verification; interpretations are not. Hypotheses must therefore be modified or discarded altogether when it becomes clear that empirical observation belies them. Interpretations, however, may remain pitted against other interpretations without necessarily voiding each other. A history of mankind told in terms of the struggle for power is neither more nor less scientific than a view of history as the development of modes of production. It is merely a different manner of interpreting the same process. The two views will yield two different stories, with quite a different distribution of highlights and obscure spots. The data will be presented in completely different arrangements; and yet, both stories may be entirely correct. Depending on the purpose, one may be more adequate or useful an interpretation than the other. But this is a pragmatic criterion which must not be confused with scientific verification. In the final analysis, all interpretation entails some arbitrary choice which cannot be defended on purely scientific grounds.

This does not mean that the social scientist should refrain from interpreting his data. On the contrary, he will contribute to scientific knowledge by doing so. But he must be careful not to insist that his interpretation is the best, or the only correct one, from the point of view of social science. He should, indeed, point out what insight his interpretation yields which others are covering up. But he should not claim that his interpretation alone is scientific.

It is perhaps because they have tended to make just this claim that Marxists have often tended to give their theory a teleological cast that far exceeds the bounds of what functional theories may properly imply. In order to show what is meant by this statement, we shall have to go back to the concept of conditioning which was discussed on pages 29–31. According to the Marxist view, the substructure does not create its superstructure; it merely predisposes the society to accommodate the development of superstructural features that are in tune with the substructure, and to slough off disfunctional features. Thus Marxism points out that a Don Quixote cannot possibly thrive in the modern age.

Now, this theory of conditioning makes sense only as long as the specific interpretation of the society as a "going concern" is plausible. It was said that the act of interpretation involves arbitrary decisions. This does not mean that any, even the most far-fetched, direction or aim may be imputed to the "going concern"; it means only that we cannot pick out one single human pursuit as the one and only, or the primary pursuit. The statement that man is adequately defined as an animal who produces is not subject to verification. He is also an animal who aims to satisfy his libido and who seeks power. Marxism is a plausible theory because man is indeed an animal that produces. It tends to be dogmatic when it regards the pursuit of economic goals as paramount, and regards all other human pursuits as incidental, and subordinate, to this economic drive. Nonetheless, Marxism is correct in realizing that in the social structure of sixteenth century Spain there was no room for the knight-errant. This does not mean that a deranged mind cannot conceive of himself as a knight-errant; the wards of our mental hospitals may harbor many a man who thinks he is God, or Napoleon, or George Washington. Such Don Quixotes, however, are bound to become the butt of everyone's joke, or end up in a hospital for the insane.

But Marxism usually goes further than that. It not only points out that dysfunctional features are bound to be sloughed off, or to be incidental to the point of ridicule. Its followers also tend to attribute creative power to the substructure. The social structure is seen not only as a negative conditioner of the superstructure; it is also said to be the creator of a superstructure that is appropriate to it. It is not only the Don Quixotes who are ground to bits between the millstones of reality; the same millstones, in the Marxist view, inevitably grind our personalities, institutions, and ideologies to fit the needs of the time. Moreover, the Marxist economic interpretation contains within itself a theory of progress: the development of man's ability to master nature never stands still. The productive forces of mankind are continuously developing into higher and higher relations of production. The progress of mankind is regarded as an inevitable trend.

This assertion seems at first glance to be a consequence of the Marxist insistence that their interpretation of man's history is the only scientific one: if the economic pursuits of mankind are paramount over all other pursuits, societies face the alternative of retrogressing or developing functional institutions, ideas, personalities, and philosophies and "hatching" new forces of production "in their loins." Yet, even given a dogmatic acceptance of the economic interpretation, it would be possible to avoid the belief in inevitable progress. One could conceive of a theory which intended to investigate all societies as going concerns organized for production. The followers of such a theory would be interested chiefly in examining all functional features, of which there are bound to be many. They would also expect to find plenty of quixotic features in a given society, and would be interested in these only as symptoms of stress and as disturbing elements. Marxism, in contrast, tends to affirm that the development of a functional superstructure is inevitable, and thus transforms the functional view into a view of causal chains. The mechanistic conception of science which Marx and Engels still had, compelled them to prove the reality of progress; and this proof could only be furnished if progress was made the end link in a causal chain. Here is the root of that animistic fallacy which we shall have to discuss in a later chapter.

Equally objectionable as this attempt to write a scientific theory of progress is the parallel claim that Marxism is also a scientific morality. The notion that socialism has been made scientific, which Engels propounded in the very title of one of his pamphlets, implies not only that the coming of socialism has been proved, but also that a socialist program of action is the only action program justified by scientific analysis. Marxism says, in short, that moral values, too, can and must be derived scientifically. All action must be based on a scientific recognition of reality, not on some eternally valid moral laws.

The admonition that action programs should be based on a scientific recognition of concrete circumstances need not conflict with the adoption of universal, absolute moral values. On the contrary, all absolutely binding moral commands must be applied to the given situation; hence a relativistic application of moral laws is perfectly reconcilable with the adoption of an absolutist concept of a moral code. Marx and Engels, however, debunked the very notion of such absolutist relativism: the scientific description of reality alone should, by inference, yield a strategy of action.

This is a demand impossible of fulfilment. A program of action, as Kant has shown convincingly, cannot be inferred from description only. The minimum of additional premises necessary for such a deduction would be at least one proposition establishing the end desired. And this proposition would not belong to the realm of description; it belongs, in final analysis, to ethics. And, indeed, if we investigate the way in which the Marxists have deduced their program of action from their description of reality, we inevitably find that, hidden under the claim to have given a scientific basis to morality, there are always some nonempirical propositions concerning the end desired. Even while they debunk the notion of morality, Marx and Engels and their followers are intensely committed to a very definite set of moral values.

But, instead of stating these values and describing how they should determine action programs under concrete circumstances, Marxism hides them behind the rigorous moral relativism it proposes. The adoption of absolute values and the description of changing circumstances is thus not resolved, as it well could be. Instead, a hidden dualism runs under the surface of Marxist theory. Moral absolutism and moral relativism, an intuitive and a pragmatic set of values, exist side by side.

We have already seen that a similar duality pervades all Marxist thought. Mechanistic and dialectical conceptions; accidentalist and teleological views; empirical and rationalist methods; they can all be found hidden in the conceptual structure of historical materialism, and the very fact that they are hidden makes the contradiction within each of the methods we have paired an unresolved problem. We are going to find more such contradictory pairs, most important among them a realistic together with a pragmatic theory of existence, and an absolutist with a relativistic conception of truth.

Little would be explained if we traced these methodological difficulties to mere confusion or incompetence on the part of Marx and Engels. Instead, we shall see that these difficulties are due to the fact that Marxism is not merely social science: it is something more, and by the same token less, than social science. It cannot be understood at all if it is seen only as an attempt to contribute to the proper recognition and description of reality even if we add a program of action supposedly deduced from this description. Instead, it has to be realized that Marxism, in addition to its very real scientific aspirations, entails two further elements that have nothing at all to do with these aspirations. It entails a political or moral attitude: radicalism. And it entails a faith which is essentially metaphysical: an unshakable belief in progress. These three aspects — the scientific aspirations, the radical criticism of reality, and the faith in progress — are essential characteristics of Marxist theory as seen by the author of this work, and no one who has dropped any one of the three can properly call himself an heir to Marx and Engels.

It is obvious that the intimate linking of these three elements is going to be reflected in the conceptual structure of Marxist scientific theory. We shall see that the unresolved contradictions which we have discovered in the method of historical materialism may be traced to these different elements of the ideology as a whole. Now, the Marxist claim is that the higher unity of science, radicalism, and faith, resolves these methodological contradictions, just as a synthesis gives functional meaning to mutually contradictory phenomena.

The plan of the following chapters is given by the statements made above. Our first step will have to be to continue our exposition of Marxist theory by describing its radicalism and its optimism. We shall end this description by showing how Marxism attempts to integrate the three component elements of its ideology, and how this integration is supposed to reconcile the methodological contradictions we have outlined. This exposition will be followed by a critical evaluation, in the course of which we shall come to the conclusion that the resolution of the contradictions has not in fact been achieved, and that, indeed, the three elements have not in fact constituted an integrated theoretical whole. Finally, we shall trace the theoretical and practical consequences of this *de facto* disintegration of Marxist ideology, as it became more and more apparent.

Chapter Two

Marx as a Radical Critic
of Civilization

The individuals always did and always do take themselves as points of departure. Their conditions are the conditions of their real life process. Whence does it come that their conditions acquire independence against themselves? that the forces of their own lives become superior forces that are turned against them?

In one word: the division of labor, the stage of which in every case depends on the development of the productive force.

As in religion man is governed by the products of his own brain, so in capitalistic production he is governed by the products of his own hand.   Karl Marx

Radical Criticism and Marxist Social Science

"The will to revolutionary activity is a condition indispensable to the understanding of Marxist dialectics." This startling sentence is attributed to Leon Trotsky by Max Eastman, who adds the sardonic comment, "All your doubts will disappear after you join the church." [1] We can safely accept Eastman's authority and take it for granted that Trotsky made this statement; for it is entirely faithful to a profound conviction held by all representative Marxists. Similar statements have been made by Engels, Lenin, and many others.[2] But, if these statements are correct, would it not be futile for any man who is not a revolutionary to try to understand Marxist theory? The present study would seem to be a wasted undertaking if the will to revolutionary activity were a precondition to an understanding of what Marx and Engels have written.

And yet, it should be possible to understand any ideology even if we cannot partake of its spirit and share its biases. Surely, we need not be mice in order to study the physiology and behavior of these little animals. We need not be converted to a strange cult if we want to dissect and reassemble its ideology. Neither do we need to be members of the Communist Party to understand the theories of Marx and Engels.

Nevertheless, if Trotsky is right, then the outsider studying Marxist theory must at least be constantly aware that this theory includes, as one of its essential elements, a revolutionary attitude, a spirit of revolt. *Marxism cannot be understood if we do not realize that radicalism is its point of departure.*

If this does not prevent the non-Marxist from studying it, it nevertheless is the chief reason why he very often feels unable to follow Marxists in their thoughts. We have pointed out in the preceding chapter that the daring connections made by brilliant Marxists, the astonishing correspondences they uncover, often leave the uninitiated social scientist with a feel of uneasiness and dissatisfaction, however strong his admiration may be for the imagination and the suggestiveness of Marxist theories. It is easy to understand this lack of communication if we realize the unbridgeable gulf which separates Marxists and non-Marxists in their political attitude. Many Marxist theorists have emphasized the resulting inability of bourgeois social scientists to grasp the insights offered by Marx and Engels, though they neglect to realize that this intellectual block will also blind the radical critic, in his turn, to certain insights. Later in this chapter we shall have to discuss this Marxist theory of ideology which is akin to the Freudian notion that the individual fiercely resists the analyst in his attempt to uncover the subconscious processes which have formed the patient's personality. The individual, according to Freudian doctrine, resists because he is afraid of the self-knowledge which analysis might open to him. Similarly, the member of the ruling class, according to Marxist doctrine, resists absorbing the knowledge offered by the radical critic of the existing order.

In a letter to his friend, Ruge, the young Marx wrote: "If

the construction of the future and the reaching of the goal for all times is not our business, then our present task is all the more certain; it means the reckless criticism of all that exists, reckless in the sense that the criticism is not afraid of its own results, and just as little of the conflict with the powers that be." [3] The fiery spirit of revolt that breathes in this passage never abated as long as Marx and Engels were alive, and it remained one of the few most essential elements of Marxist ideology, pervading everything the two men wrote. Once the Marxist movement ceases to be radical, the letter of Marxism may be upheld, but its spirit disappears. In one of their early joint works, Marx and Engels emphasized the necessity "to oppose all phrases which might weaken or water down the consciousness of the total opposition of Communism against the existing world today." [4] A would-be Marxist who is not a radical critic of his environment would surely be disavowed by the founders of the movement, were they still alive.

Ever since the rise of right-wing totalitarian movements that call for a "conservative revolution," the word "radicalism" has acquired a far broader meaning than it had in the nineteenth century. For those who would call national-socialists, fascists, and Silver-shirters radical, the word has come to mean any violent, coercive, destructive reaction to political and social disappointment. It might even be used to characterize the mood of a lynching mob. It is impatience, proneness to violence, and intense antidemocratic feelings; it is, in short, the method of action of all those rebellious elements in contemporary society who react sharply against a general social and political malaise.

The radicalism of Marx and Engels and their followers does in fact imply all the intensity of feeling and action that is characteristic of extremism in all political camps (though we shall see that something more is implied in the radicalism of the Marxist movement). Militancy, impatience, and ruthlessness make up this maximalism, which Lenin once characterized in the following words:

. . . the Marxist, making full use of *any* — even reactionary — *soil* for the struggle for revolution, does not sink down to an apotheosis of reaction and does not forget about the fight for the *best possible ground* on which to act. Therefore the Marxist *is the first* to foresee the coming of the revolutionary era and starts to waken the people and ring the bell already at a time when the philistines still dream the slavish dream of loyal subjects. Therefore the Marxist *is the first* to enter the road of outright revolutionary struggle, to go into direct battle, exposing the appeasement illusions of all social and political mediocrities. For the same reason the Marxist *is the last* to leave the road of directly-revolutionary struggle, and leaves it only when all possibilities are exhausted, when there is not even the shadow of hope for a shorter road, when the call to prepare for mass strikes, for rebellion, and so forth, obviously loses ground.[5]

The reader will have noted the intimate connection which Lenin, in the above passage, draws between radical action and an analysis of the actual situation. This recalls the Marxist assertion that their radicalism is scientific, an assertion with which we dealt at the end of the preceding chapter. In theory at least, the Leninist who calls for a revolutionary uprising does so only when he is convinced that the situation is ripe for an uprising. The Marxist who demands the substitution of a socialist order for the present social structure and social institutions claims that his prescription for curing the ills of mankind is scientific because it is a realistic prescription. Their program, said Marx and Engels, was not utopian because it was based on the real possibilities or potentialities inherent in the present situation.

It was pointed out toward the end of Chapter 1 that this realistic approach to problems of action, proper as it is, does not make programs of action scientific. A preconceived notion of what is and what is not desirable must be at the basis of all calculations by which action programs are derived. The radicalism of Marx and Engels is just this value judgment which underlies their entire social thought and political action; and here we have radicalism as the term was understood before the First World War. At that time it did not so much characterize the rebellious mood and the violent methods, but referred more specifically to the aims set forth by rebel leaders. Specifically, it meant the desire to extend political and social democracy as much as possible; the wish to abolish all inequalities; the uncompromising demand for liberty, both in the positive and negative sense. The nineteenth-century radical asks that a clean sweep be made of all oppressive features in the social structure, of all oppressive institutions, and that the very atmosphere of the culture be cleansed of oppressiveness. Stressing the positive side of liberty, the radical of the old type asserts that man can stand on his own feet, and that he can make his own history, if only he could free himself of self-deception, myths, and intellectual opiates. It is, basically, an intense and exclusive *humanism,* which demands the destruction of all institutions that are unworthy of man, and the construction of a society worthy of this highest creation. Marx expressed this radical humanism very early in his life when he wrote: "A critique of religion leads to the doctrine that *the highest being for man is man himself,* hence to the categorical imperative to overthrow all relationships in which man is humbled, enslaved, abandoned, despised." [6]

It need hardly be pointed out that this radical humanism is a direct continuation of the Christian-Humanist-Democratic tradition of our civilization. Marx, with his humanist critique of civilization, is a direct heir of Jan Hus, Thomas Moore, Thomas Paine, and Jean-Jacques Rousseau.

It is inevitable that this value orientation affect the scientific findings of historical materialism. Marxist social science is not merely a description of reality; it is throughout a *critical* description of reality. This tends to make it, at best, a one-sided description; for, given the critical attitude, the Marxist is prone to pick out only those features in society which can be criticized. Harping on what is wrong with civilization, he is likely to exaggerate the significance of objectionable features. This is decidedly a feature which detracts from the scientific validity of Marxist sociology. On the other hand, the radical-humanist orientation is intimately connected with the most modern aspects of the Marxist view. To show what is meant, we had best quote Marx himself, who wrote: "To be radical means to grab the matter by its root. But the root of man is man himself." The phrase is so pithy it might seem obscure. Obviously, the radicalism to which Marx refers here is not an attitude; Marx, in calling himself a radical, is not inferring that he criticizes institutions. Instead, he is critical in the Kantian sense of the word. That means that he aims to subject his methods of analysis to a radical critique.[7] And this critical method leads him to the sensible conclusion of contemporary social anthropology, that culture is the product of the interaction of human beings, a proposition which does not strike us as remarkable, but which was decidedly radical in the 1840's. What the modern social anthropologist would regard as controversial in the Marxian position is not the method to which it leads but the derivation of this anthropological method from a radical attitude. For, although the word "radical" in the sentence quoted from Marx has a methodological meaning (to go to the roots of reality), the word remains ambiguous. Surely this ambiguity was intended. For Marxism links a method which goes to the roots of reality, a method which dispels illusions and fantasies about the world, with an attitude that attacks and debunks the present world at its very roots. In his scientific method as well as in his political attitude toward reality, Marx aims to be a radical debunker, and this aim leads him to the statement that a radical, critical attitude is the precondition of a critical scientific method. Radicalism, says Marx, is scientifically correct.

This is only another aspect of the Marxist claim to have made morality scientific. If socialism is scientific, then certainly the critique of the capitalist social structure, from which socialism as an aim is derived, must be scientific. If it is scientific to demand a better world, then it must be equally scientific to criticize the existing world. We have, however, pointed out that there cannot be such a thing as a scientific morality. This means, therefore, that a critical attitude, too, can never be supported on scientific grounds. And, if we take a look at Marxist statements in this regard, we shall see that Marxism has not succeeded in its attempt to throw a scientific cloak around the radical attitude.

Here we shall discuss only one of these attempts, the interpretation of dialectics in a radically critical sense. Dialectics had provided concepts which symbolized a reality in continual conflict and continual change. It had emphasized the creative results of struggle, showing a decided spirit of relativism and ephemerality, and an awareness that nothing is eternal. All Marx and Engels had to do was to give a positive evaluation to their description of reality, very much in the manner of Hegel who had said that everything which is real is reasonable. Engels merely reverses this statement by saying: "Everything that is real within the realm of the history of mankind is bound to become unreasonable after a while; hence it is already by definition unreasonable, is afflicted with unreasonableness from the very beginning; . . . Everything that exists deserves to perish." [8] The spirit of radical criticism could not be expressed with greater sharpness. Engels himself feels the urge to make it clear that this interpretation of dialectics inevitably leads to radical conclusions:

> Just as the bourgeoisie, by means of big industry, competition, and the world market, dissolves all stable, old-established, venerable institutions in practice, so dialectical philosophy dissolves all imaginations of ultimate absolute truth and absolute conditions of mankind corresponding to them. Before it nothing ultimate, nothing absolute or holy stands up; of everything and in everything it points out the passing character. . . . True, it has its conservative aspect, too; for it recognizes the legitimacy of definite stages of knowledge and social organization for the times and circumstances corresponding to them, but only as far as that. The conservatism of this type of view is relative, its revolutionary character is absolute — *the only absolute thing it leaves valid*.[9]

As it turned out, little remained of conservatism in Marxist dialectics; the revolutionary character remained absolute. The paradox situation developed that this doctrine of the process of change, which should be so much more aware of the flow of time than other theories, tended to neglect the time element unduly, so that it served to justify the boundless impatience which is part of Marxist radicalism. The actual duration of processes is far too concrete to be expressed by the abstractions of dialectics. Each moment of time is seen in the context of the totality of past and future, and this tends to rob the moment, or any time span, of all significance. On the one hand, therefore, Marxist politicians viewing the present *sub specie aeternitatis* could conceivably console themselves that socialism would be victorious in an indeterminate future. The unsatisfactory present is glorified by the vision of a future when this vision is conjured up with such intensity that nothing but the promise of better days is seen in the present. Here we have a methodological justification of the conservatism and complacency of the Soviet regime.[10] But, where Marxism is still a movement of rebellion, the futurism[11] of dialectics takes the form of that intense impatience which we have characterized as one element of Marxist radicalism. Future tasks are seen immediately at hand, and all the world's ills must be removed at one stroke. Each moment is given decisive significance. Every moment's action is seen as the crucial act of deliverance. Time must not interfere.

It has already been pointed out that this radicalism affects the descriptive part of Marxism, its analysis of society. This takes two forms. First, futurism implies a preoccupation with things as they will be, or as they ought to be, a preoccupation with trends of development which has often turned into wishful thinking, however much wishes or desires are disclaimed. When Engels writes that "everything that is reasonable *within the heads of men* is destined to become real, however much it may contradict the existing seeming reality," [12] he makes his vision of the future, his idea of what it would be reasonable to achieve, appear more real than the stubborn facts which are only seemingly real. This idealism (in the Marxist sense) of Engels was later incorporated systematically into Leninism, where the most important and the most real driving force of history is revealed as the consciousness of a handful of professional revolutionaries originating in the bourgeoisie.[13] To be sure, this consciousness is said to be a reflection of reality, hence devoid of any "idealism." But Lenin was as eager as Engels to describe his vision of the future as more real than the present:

> The men'sheviks . . . take only the first half of Hegel's well-known statement that "all that is real is reasonable, all that is reasonable is real." The Duma is real. That means, the Duma is reasonable, they say, and are satisfied with that. The fight outside the Duma is "reasonable," we reply. It springs with objective necessity out of the entire contemporary situation. That means it is "real," even though it is suppressed at the present moment.[14]

Secondly, as has been pointed out, Marxist description is critical description. And the remainder of this chapter will be devoted to an exposition of the entire critique of civilization which Marx and Engels have made. We shall examine how they think present institutions and social relationships came into existence and why they are unworthy of man.

The Theory of Alienation

Marxism, wrote Engels in his polemic against Eugen Dühring, is a modification and elaboration of Rousseau's *Essay on the Origin of Inequality*.[15] Indeed, Marxism not only describes antagonistic and exploitative relationships that are expressed in the class struggle which racks every society; it has also attempted to trace the origin of all class-divided society as such. And, just as Rousseau posited a noble savage who preceded civilization and its ills, so the Marxist scheme of development begins with the description of a golden age of innocence: primitive tribal society. In conformity with the scientific aspirations of Marx and Engels, this conception of the golden age is based on the research of a social scientist, Lewis Morgan, an American anthropologist who had made field studies among the Iroquois Indians. Many statements made by Morgan have not been corroborated, and a good deal of the Engelsian interpretation of his findings is highly controversial. Thus the Marxist view of the golden age of primitive communism is not borne out by social science. Nevertheless it is important to become familiar with this view, as it serves as the point of departure for the entire Marxist theory of alienation, the theory which seeks to explain the processes by which mankind has drifted further and further away from the original state of innocence.

Naturally, Marxist theory seizes on the mode of production in its attempt to tell this development of civilization. In describing primitive communist society, Engels points out the rudimentary level of technological and sociological development that characterizes it. The productive knowledge of primitive man, who has not even an inkling of what full mastery over nature might provide, is severely restricted. Nature is still a terrifying force, with inscrutable laws or whims. Primitive man therefore leads a precarious hand-to-mouth existence, producing only the absolute necessities for a barbaric way of life. His social organization is functionally related to this mode of production; that means the level of production and the social organization correspond (Engels, however, says that they can be seen as causes and effects of each other). The striking features of primitive society, as Engels imagined it, were its liberty and its equality, not only a negative equality in misery, but a more fundamental equality of production. There being no surplus, there could be no inequality of distribution. But, in the eyes of Engels, primitive society had not yet developed a division of labor. Its production was not only social, but also communal. This communal character of production, not the primitive level of technology, was the essence of primitive communism in the eyes of Marx and Engels. Long before Engels wrote his interpretation of Lewis Morgan's work, Marx and Engels had stated very clearly that the division of labor was, to them, the surest indication of the development of the forces of production.[16]

Not only production, but also appropriation, was communal in primitive society as depicted by Marx and Engels. All products, including the means of production, were communal property, so that there was no property system at all. For this reason, primitive society could know no leisure class, no exploiters, indeed no classes whatsoever, not even slaves. Prisoners-of-war, Engels wrote, were either eaten or were incorporated into the tribe. Since the primitive development of the forces of production compelled all members of society to work as much as they could, slavery would have made no sense.[17]

To Marx and Engels, as well as to Lewis Morgan, these features carried with them a surprising amount of freedom, both in the sense of positive freedom — for primitive society was closely knit, well integrated, and encouraged the development of each individual's fullest potentialities on a primitive level — and in the sense of negative freedom — for there was no oppression or exploitation. Primitive society, then, was seen as a spontaneously integrated community with a real general will, in which each contributed according to his ability and received according to what the whole society produced. True, production was on the narrowest possible scale, but, to quote Engels, "it entailed the producer's mastery over their process of production and its product. . . . As long as production is carried on on this basis it cannot grow over the producers' heads, cannot beget any monstrous foreign power facing them, as is regularly and inevitably the case in civilization." [18]

"That," he writes in the same volume, "was the tremendous advantage of barbarous production, which was lost with the advent of civilization, and which to regain (though on the basis of man's newly gained tremendous mastery of nature and the free association now possible) will be the task of the next generation." [9]

The warm, glowing tone Engels uses, and the naïve envy that speaks in this passage should not cause the reader to forget that his admiration for primitive tribal society was not undivided. After all, the agreeable features of primitive communism were bound up with the barbarously primitive level of production; hence, if there was no oppression of man by his fellow-men, there was, instead, his abject dependence on the whims and forces of nature.

The subsequent "growth of the forces of production," [20] which ended the stage of primitive communism, is therefore considered as a progressive step in the history of mankind, a step toward that full mastery over nature which, according to Marxism, is one of the preconditions for a truly human history, a history free from all concern over the production of life's necessities. And yet, the growth of the forces of production, according to Marx and Engels, was not altogether a good thing; for the time being, at least, this growth of man's productive forces, which is the growth of civilization, has brought with it a number of evil features which, as a matter of fact, have become more and more intensified as civilization progresses.

Students of Marxist writings have not, in the past, recognized sufficiently the profound kinship between Marxism and German romanticism in their criticism of civilization. Marx centered his critique on different aspects of modern living, and the political conclusions he drew were entirely opposed to anything offered by the romantics. But, like them, he came to the general conclusion that modern civilization was antihuman or inhuman, that it was unworthy of man's inherent qualities and potentialities. Like them, he posited a noble and intelligent human species, whose goodness and intelligence are frustrated by the process of civilization. Like the romantic critics of bourgeois society, Marx asserted that men have become *alienated* both from their environment and from their own selves. This concept of alienation, of crucial importance to the Marxist critique, has been taken directly from the vocabulary of German romanticism. It means that man has been severed or removed from his natural environment, so that his relationship to the environment of which he is an organic part is no longer as immediate or intimate as it used to be. And, as self-alienation, it means also that man has been stunted and perverted and become something less than a real human being.

(Man, according to the Marxist view, no longer moves in the natural environment which was familiar to the primitive tribe. He has created barriers between himself and nature: tools, machines, and an entire artificial way of urban living. The more he has mastered the forces of nature, the more he has become estranged from the natural environment.⸰ But the division of labor, which develops in step with technological progress, also erects an artificial social barrier between man and nature. Man's growing mastery over the forces of nature goes hand in hand with the development of the class struggle. In the words of Marx: "The very moment civilization begins, production begins to be founded on the antagonism of orders, estates, classes, and finally on the antagonism of accumulated labor [that is, the products of man's labor: goods and tools] and actual labor. No antagonism, no progress. This is the law that civilization has followed up to our own days." [21] This class structure creates, as it were, a second nature which, according to Marxism, begins to rule the producers in proportion to the degree that society advances technologically.

A strange phrase occurred in the passage we quoted from Marx, "the antagonism of accumulated labor and actual labor." This points to a further feature of alienation as described in Marxist theory: the notion that the division of labor serves to alienate labor from its tools when another class controls the essential means of production and communication. And, since the means of production are themselves products of labor, Marx can say that past labor rules over living labor. What he means to say is that exploitative relationships are not natural but are creations of mankind itself, by-products of the growth of civilization, features of alienation.

When Marx uses the term "exploitation," he points to another feature of man's alienation in class society: Labor, he says, is separated from its product, because a special class that controls the means of production appropriates the product of surplus labor, leaving the laborer only the product of that necessary labor which he must expend in order to produce the barest means for his continued existence. Thus the growth of society's productive forces beyond the most primitive level is seen as the indirect cause of the domination of men by men, of class differences and class subjugation.

Furthermore, the Marxist theory of alienation holds that all natural, spontaneous relationships between men have been corroded and perverted by being cast into the rigid shells of oppressive institutions. A free and spontaneous relationship between the sexes and between the generations is made impossible by the various types of family organization, one as oppressive and unnatural as the other. The natural brotherhood of all men is stifled by divisive loyalties to tribes, monarchs, and nations. And instead of a communal general will, a natural and spontaneous unanimity of purpose and implementation, there is the state. In short, the entire superstructure of institutions and relationships that exist on top of the division of labor and the class structure is something which Marxism not only describes, but also criticizes and condemns. Marx wants to abolish not only the division of labor and the existence of classes. He also wants the entire superstructure of family, law, nation, and state to wither away.[22] Like Rousseau and the romantics, he seems to believe that all political and human relations can take natural spontaneous forms. And, as we shall see, he also subscribes to the notion of a productive human intellect unfettered by superstition and methodological inadequacies. These are also, in the final analysis, parts of the evil superstructure.

How, in the Marxist view, did this superstructure come into being? Marx sees civilized society torn from its natural environment and alienated within itself. The process of production which, under primitive communism, tied the society together into a harmonious community now acts as an agent of corrosion and a cause of tensions. This tension, however, is not one that will cause society to break into pieces; on the contrary, a given class society is a functioning organism only because of its very antagonisms, tensions, and struggles. If one or the other class in a given class society were to disappear, the society would simply dissolve. Modern industry without workers, ancient Athens without its slaves, feudal manors without peasants would be unthinkable.

Nonetheless, the class societies of the Marxian scheme must be thought of as constantly torn by virulent class war, as constantly on the verge of revolutionary upheaval. To mitigate this serious social disequilibrium, Marxism sees an entire apparatus of institutions and ideas arise to keep society together. This apparatus, which it calls the superstructure, comprises the legal system, a system of approved kinship relations, mores, beliefs concerning the nature of the universe, theories of society, political institutions, and even schools of art, and is seen in a specific ancillary relationship to a society's class structure and mode of production. Each and every one of the elements of the superstructure is a means, unconsciously and spontaneously devised by society, to keep itself integrated in its present class structure. The superstructure, therefore, seemingly mitigates the struggle between the classes, because it aims to make the present class structure more palatable to the exploited classes, to turn their eyes away from the class struggle and to obscure its very existence. By that same token, however, it is a very direct weapon in the class struggle because it serves the conservative interests of the ruling classes.

The best known application of the theory of superstructure is the Marxist theory of the state. According to Engels it arises out of class conflict. "A product of society at a certain stage of its development, it is the admission that this society has become entangled in an insoluble contradiction with itself, that it is cleft into irreconcilable antagonisms which it is powerless to dispel." [23] Translated into the language of Hobbes and Rousseau, this means that, according to Engels, the state can exist only if and as long as it has the worms of corporations in its bowels. It cannot, therefore, be the expression of a general will; were there a general will, there would be no state.

So much for the origin of the state. As for its nature, the

Marxist theory considers it to be the institution through which class relationships and the class struggle manifest themselves as power relationships. It is the control center or decision-making apparatus of society, underneath which the social structure remains as a subconscious driving force and conditioner of the will. Engels, therefore, compared the state to the brains of society: "As in the individual all driving forces of his action go through his head and must be transformed into motives of his will in order to make him act, so all the wants of civic society — no matter what class is ruling at a given moment — must pass through the will of the state in order to receive general validity in the form of laws." [24]

The basic function of this brain center, according to Engels, is to maintain society alive by developing and enforcing — enforcing even against recalcitrant or deviant members of the ruling classes — a system of rules of behavior. As Engels put it, "in order to prevent these antagonisms — classes with conflicting economic interests — from consuming themselves and society in fruitless struggle, a power seemingly standing above society has become necessary which is to mitigate the conflict, to keep it within the bounds of 'order'; and this power, originating in society but placing itself above society and alienating itself more and more from it, is the state." [25] But, since the state is an instrument to keep society going in its present form, an instrument designed to formalize and perpetuate the existing class structure and property relations, it becomes automatically beneficial to the ruling classes; and in that sense only does it turn into the "executive committee" of these classes; and to the extent that the rule of those classes is obsolete and oppressive, the state is regarded as a fetter of the forces of production. Moreover, the state, as a superstructural feature, can acquire a dynamics of its own and become an end in itself. Marx's favorite examples of states that have become ends in themselves were the Second Empire of Napoleon III and the Prussian Junker state; both were, in his eyes, parasitic systems exploiting society and keeping it impotent by making use of the antagonism of classes. In that sense, Engels could call the state the organ of "public power distinct from the mass of the people." [26]

Another word for these dynamics of its own which superstructural things can and do acquire, according to Marxist theory, is *lag*. The concept of lag in Marxist usage denotes the development of a dysfunctional relationship, a noncorrespondence, between the substructure and the superstructure. Under the impact of technological change, or corresponding with it, the social structure changes; and, as the basic social structure changes, the entire superstructure of political and legal institutions, attitudes, mores, and traditions of the society changes too. But, says Marx, the superstructure changes at a different pace, and the assumption is that this is a slower pace.

This can be explained as the result of a certain inertia that may be inherent in formal institutions or formalized social relationships. Form becomes a fetter to content. By being cast into the form of institutions, men's social relationships lag behind the actual development of the social structure. The forms become aims in themselves. But it can also be explained as a result of the actions of conservative men, who seek by all possible means to perpetuate the social relations in which they have a vested interest, even though these social relations no longer correspond to the actual process of production. The privileges of the landed aristocracy in France had long ceased to contribute to the development of the forces of production; on the contrary, they were sapping the country's resources. Yet it took years of violent and bloody revolution before the superstructure of a bygone mode of production had been smashed, so that a free-enterprise economy could develop freely.

In short, the concept of lag denotes that the institutional and ideological superstructure, though closely related to the substructure of economic relationships, lags behind the development of the productive apparatus and can thus exert a drag on the progress of society as a whole.[27] More generally, lag implies the recognition that man's actions exert an unwanted influence long after they have been committed. Man's creations assume an independent influence of their own and can even come to rule over their creators, as in capitalism, which Marx once defined as the "command of the product of past labor over living surplus labor" and as "that specific social relationship in which past labor confronts living labor independently and overpoweringly." [28] Lag is, then, the discrepancy between purpose and result, or the difference between man's making use of his environment, with unexpected results, and man's mastery of his environment.

The concept of lag has been criticized as an intellectual subterfuge, that is, a device by which to rescue an intrinsically untenable theory of economic determinism. Of course, the concept is an implicit admission that the economic substructure does not directly determine the superstructure as cause determines effect. All deviations from a strict and unbending determinism of this sort can thus be explained away, even though the theory of economic determinism — in the final analysis — might still be defended. Precisely for this reason, the concept of lag has been criticized as unscientific, most sharply perhaps by Karl Popper, who claims that a hypothesis which cannot be challenged successfully has no place in a scientific theory. Of course, Karl Popper is quite right if our conception of scientific theory is a mechanistic one, investigating cause-and-effect relationships, and working with hypotheses. Engel's statement that in the final analysis economic processes do determine the superstructure, lends support to the understanding that this was his conception of scientific method, too. But, if we are correct in explaining the economic interpretation of history as a functional view, Popper's criticism misses the mark. Not because Popper criticizes the economic interpretation of Marxism; he is, on the contrary, quite justified in questioning why this particular aspect of life should have been singled out as the central functional coëfficient. His criticism does miss the mark, however, because he mistakes the functional for the cause-and-effect view which could not operate at all with the concept of lag, whatever the central functional coëfficient.

Finally, Marxist theory says nothing concrete about any features of the superstructure, including that of the state. Hence it does not claim to be political science, jurisprudence, sociology, or any other discipline. On the contrary, Marxism claims that all the disciplines, in developing universally applicable theories of state, law, or any other institution, do violence to the doctrine that features of the superstructure must be seen in relation to the underlying class structure and class struggle, that "every form of production creates its own legal relations, forms of government, etc." [29] In the broadest terms, the superstructure is nothing more than a complex and perpetually changing array of means by which society maintains and regulates its present division of labor. But, Marx and Engels point out, the superstructural nature of politics, law, culture, and ideology has, so far, been obscured. More often than not political relationships have been thought to be the mainsprings of the productive process, instead of being merely one of its secondary aspects. Man's productive labor, which has in the final analysis created the entire superstructure, seems, on the contrary, to be determined by it. Effects are mistaken for causes; epiphenomena, for the realities themselves.

With this we have come to a final feature of alienation: the Marxist notion that the process of civilization has perverted and stifled man's intelligence, his ability to recognize reality. But we shall postpone a discussion of this *theory of ideology* and its implications. At this time we shall, instead, complement the Marxist view of man in alienation by the more concrete criticism of modern capitalist society.

The Theory of Capitalism

Following closely in the footsteps of the Romantic critics, Marx and Engels saw in bourgeois society the peak of man's alienation from himself. The means of production, perfected by man for the purpose of attaining mastery over nature, have now, according to this theory, assumed mastery over man. The tools have developed their own rules of the game, and human life is adjusted to the requirements of production as dictated by the tools rather than by man's reason.

Let us trace individual features of this alienation as seen by Marxist theory. For one thing, under capitalist conditions, production is separated from use. Feudal and slave societies supposedly produced articles for direct consumption. Capitalism is production for the purpose of selling the product on the market at a profit; it is the production of commodities for the sake of increasing capital. Quite appropriately, therefore, *Das Kapital* opens with a discussion of commodity production. The point Marx makes here against the classical economists is that production has not always been for the market; commodity production is only one of several possible systems of exchange, which has its history and its origins. "Exchange has a history of its own. It has passed through different phases," he had written in his tract against Proudhon. "There was a time, as in the Middle Ages, when only the superfluity, the excess of production over consumption, was exchanged. There was again a time when not only the superfluity, but all products, all industrial existence, had passed into commerce, when the whole of production depended on exchange . . . marketable value at its second power." [30] This view has been largely accepted; and the controversies between Marxists and non-Marxists now concern the question of how commodity production emerged from the feudal production-for-consumption. While Max Weber posited a spirit of capitalism, and Schumpeter referred to the "thrift and brains" of pioneer entrepreneurs, Marxists have weighed the relative importance of forces internal to the feudal world and outside influences, like the influx of commodities and bullion due to the crusades, to piracy, trade, and the great discoveries; finally, the effect of all such influences on the social structure. [31]

The great stress laid on the analysis of commodity production in *Das Kapital* and previous works points to the fact that the starting point of the Marxian analysis is not production but exchange. [32] This explains Marx's use of the concept of value; as used by him this concept symbolizes the recognition that capitalist production is production for the market, where commodities are exchanged against each other according to a general system of evaluation. As Sweezy points out in *The Theory of Capitalist Development*, the law of value is a theory of general equilibrium developed in commodity production which regulates not only the exchange ratios among commodities, but also determines the quantity that is to be produced of each, and the allocation of the labor force to the various branches of production. For, as Marx wrote in 1868, "every child knows . . . that the mass of products corresponding to the different needs require different and quantitatively determined masses of the total labor of society. That this necessity of distributing social labor in definite proportions cannot be done away with by the *particular form* of social production, but can only change the *form it assumes*, is self-evident. No natural law can be done away with. What can change, in changing historical circumstances, is the *form* in which these laws operate. And the form in which this particular division of labor operates in a state of society where the interconnection of social labor is manifested in the *private exchange* of the individual products of labor, is precisely the *exchange value* of these products." [33] In Marxism, thus, the theory of value leads directly to a theory of labor allocation (the division of labor), because value, according to Marx's definition, can be expressed only in terms of labor. Hence we can, true enough, repeat that the starting point of the analysis of capitalism is exchange; *but the emphasis is on the social organization of production.*

The axiom that only human labor creates value does not mean that things, natural objects to which no human labor has been added, cannot be valuable (useful). All it means is that the Marxist theory of capitalism drops considerations of utility out of sight;[34] if at all, the influence of demand on the market is mentioned only as a disturbing variable which is not, however, essential to an understanding of the mainsprings of the economic system. Both demand and supply are really seen as superstructural to the social system; ". . . absolutely nothing can be explained by the relation of supply and demand unless the basis has first been ascertained on which this relation rests." [35] On the face of it, there is nothing wrong with this procedure, as long as the existence of the minor variable is not forgotten. But it is even more important to realize that this scant regard for the function of utility and demand has a reason: the classical economists were out to discover the laws that determine the exchange value (price) of commodities. Marx condemns this approach to economic problems as fetishism.[36] Behind every commodity, he asserts, the capitalist system hides human relationships, a division of labor, an exploitative system, and a class antagonism. These social relations of capitalism, of which the commodity market is regarded as only a manifestation, are the object of his enquiry. *Hence, even while Marx is taking the market as his point of departure, he is really writing sociology, not economics.*[37] His basic disagreements with classical economics are not so much over their findings or even their concepts (which he accepted and used) as over the major goal of their research.[38]

Here we have the reason why Marx could so ingeniously turn the labor theory of value, used throughout by classical economists, into a critique of capitalist exploitation which was simple enough to have caught the imagination of millions.[39] Briefly, Marx treats the relationship between the owner of the factory and the worker as an exchange relationship. The labor market is a place where labor power is purchased as if it were a commodity; and, according to Marx, *it is in fact a commodity.* In giving the capitalist the right to use his labor power as he sees fit, the worker is, in effect, selling himself to the capitalist, though only for a contractually limited time; moreover, he is free not to sell himself at all. These two important features clearly distinguish him from the slave.

Given this freedom of the worker to sell himself; and further, the contractual nature of this exchange transaction, how can Marx speaks of exploitation? For, if average market conditions are assumed, the capitalist will certainly not be able to pay less for the commodity "labor" than its value, and it would be foolish to expect him to pay more. As a matter of fact, Marx does not claim that the laborer selling himself receives less than his value as a commodity. "The value of labor power [he writes] is determined, as in the case of every other commodity, by the labor time necessary for the production and consequently also the reproduction of this special article. . . . Given the individual, the production of labor power consists in his reproduction of himself or his maintenance." Hence, "the value of labor power is the value of the means of subsistence necessary for the maintenance of the laborer." [40] That the capitalist buys labor at exactly its value, by giving the laborer a subsistence wage, is precisely what Marx asserts. He makes no attempt to assert that the worker is cheated in the labor contract. Exploitation sets in only when the production process begins. It results from the fact that the worker, upon hiring himself to the capitalist, produces more than the value of his labor power (which he receives as his just wage). That this takes place is reflected in the simple fact that the average entrepreneur operates at a profit. He expends his capital for real property, machinery, material, and labor. Set to work in the production process, these yield him commodities, which he sells on the market. If the assumption is correct that commodities are, on the average, sold at their values, he is selling more value than he originally bought. And this excess value, according to Marx, can have been created by nothing else than the workers' labor power.[41]

Now it is clear why Marx could assert that alienation goes further under capitalism than under any previous mode of production. Not only is production separated from use, as it is in any system of commodity production; labor is also separated from appropriation, as in the days of slavery or serfdom. The precapitalist artisan in systems of simple commodity production produced for the market; he did, however, not only own the essential means of production (his workshop, tools, and raw materials), but also appropriated the product of his own labor. Deprived of his tools when he exchanged his artisan's shop for the capitalist factory, the worker is also denied title to the product of his labor. Instead, the capitalist, who owns the means of production, also appropriates the product, while the laborer is given a fixed wage. Thus human labor itself has turned into a commodity.[42] As Marx wrote in eloquent wrath: "There came a time when everything that men had considered as inalienable became an object of exchange, of traffic, and could be alienated. This is the time when the very things which till then had been communicated but never exchanged, given but never sold, acquired but never bought — virtue, love, conviction, knowledge, conscience, etc. — when everything, in short, passed into commerce. It is the time of general corruption, of universal venality, or, to speak in terms of political economy, the time when everything, moral or physical, having become a marketable value, is brought to the market to be assessed at its truest value . . . — marketable value at its third power." [43]

Not the system of exchange (commodity production), then, characterizes capitalism, but the fact that the social relations of production and *all social relationships in general have turned into exchange relationships.* Capitalism, in the words of Marx and Engels, has "dissolved all natural-organic relationships into money relationships." Hence its most essential feature is the use of free labor, and in tracing the origins and development of this mode of production, Marxism traces the process by which labor was freed from its patriarchal ties to nature or society — freed only to be forced to sell its own labor power under the most inhuman conditions.[44] Labor has been freed only to become an adjunct of the machine.

The mere quantity of labor functions as a measure regardless of quality . . . simple labor has become the pivot of industry . . . labor has been equalized by the subordination of man to the machine or by the extreme division of labor; . . . men are effaced by their labor; . . . the pendulum of the clock has become as accurate a measure of the relative activity of two workers as it is of the speed of two locomotives. . . . Time is everything, man is nothing; . . . Quality no longer matters. Quantity alone decides everything.[45]

To Marx and Engels, this *reification* (Verdinglichung) of all human qualities and human relationships was surely the *ne plus ultra* of man's alienation from himself. The entire capitalist system was seen as a huge market developing its own laws independent of man's intentions or rational plans. Even while man emancipated his reason from the fetters of superstition, mankind became utterly dependent on this superhuman second nature it had itself created. Each individual was no more than a cog in this huge mechanism, at best a specialist in a restricted field, but in any case unable to survey the entire process. Hence there could be no effective calculation or planning in advance; the balancing of needs and consumption could be accomplished only through the medium of self-adjusting social processes (the market), and in the inevitable cases of malfunction, a crisis had to right the balance, a crisis that would take on the appearance of a natural catastrophe. In the realm of thought, fetishism was the natural result of this reification process.

The Theory of Ideology

With this we have come to that aspect of man's alienation from himself to which Marx and Engels paid more attention, perhaps, than to any other: the effect of the division of classes on man's intelligence. If we can ascribe Marxist social thought to any one discipline of the social sciences, we could say that, foremost, Marxism is a *historical sociology of knowledge*, a theory of ideology which analyzes the way in which the development of civilization has falsified man's consciousness, and which points out the road by which true consciousness is bound to emerge triumphant.

It is easy to see that men alienated from their true nature and their full potentialities, men caught in the fetters of specialization and exploitation, are bound to have their intelligence stunted and frustrated. Moreover, our entire thinking process is shaped by the world in which we live. Concepts are necessarily abstracted from our own store of empirical knowledge; hypotheses are based on our past experience. Thought, therefore, can never transcend reality. In the Hegelian phrase quoted by Engels, "consciousness is conscious being" (*Bewusstsein ist bewusstes Sein*).[46] A man's thinking is determined by his entire life's situation, including his social position. But, since everyone's position in a class society is as untenable as that society itself, all consciousness in past history cannot but have been false consciousness, or self-deception. Yet, even while it is false, it is still the true reflection of the given class structure.

This word "reflection" is, like so many other terms of the Marxist vocabulary, ambiguous and misleading, for it refers to two aspects of knowledge. According to the Marxist view, ideas, concepts, and images, that is, all the mental forms which knowledge takes are reflections of reality, reflections of the objective world within which the individual lives. This realistic theory of knowledge must be sharply separated from the other theory of reflection according to which knowledge is a reflection of the individual's place within the division of labor and the class structure. In this context, the word "reflection" means no more than that knowledge corresponds to the individual's class position. The division of labor shapes the whole man: his outlook on reality, the questions he asks and the questions he leaves unasked, the frame of references through which he views the world, the things that strike him and the things that escape his notice—all this, in the Marxist view, cannot but be affected by man's role within the given class structure. No more is implied by the word "reflection" in this context. But the fact that Marxist writers have not distinguished the two theories of reflection with sufficient sharpness has made for a good deal of confusion. This confusion is particularly disturbing because the two theories of reflection can become mutually contradictory. The concept of knowledge as a reflection of reality carries with it the notion that, even though our knowledge of the world is not absolutely correct, nevertheless the element of reality is greater than the distortions. The underlying optimism of this mechanistic theory of knowledge is quite different from the implicit skepticism which, in Marxist writings, is breathed by the theory that ideas reflect the individual's restricted role in a structured society.

This Marxist theory of ideology goes back to a notion that was already familiar to the Sophists and had been revived in the eighteenth century: all thoughts and ideas are reflections of pleasure and pain, advantage and disadvantage, in short, of self-interest. Naturally, in Marxism this self-interest expresses itself as class interest. In this sense, too, all ideological phenomena are seen to correspond with the prevailing class structure. The entire climate of opinion, the premises on which most of society seems to agree, the problems being dealt with by social scientists and philosophers, the problems that are being overlooked, and the entire system of social, philosophical, and political schools—all this is regarded as superstructure to the socio-economic system and is generally traced to the conservative or reactionary desires of the ruling classes.[47]

Viewing itself and its society through distorting ideological spectacles, the ruling class, in the Marxist view, also forces its ideology on society as a whole, including the exploited classes, so that the working classes, too, are prevented from recognizing their own class interests. All of society is caught in the net of false consciousness without being aware of it. "The fact that the material conditions of life of the men in whose heads this thought process goes on determine the course of this process in the final analysis, this fact necessarily remains unknown to these men. For otherwise all ideology would come to an end."[48]

Applying this theory of ideology, Marx and Engels believed that the validity of ideas could be criticized by tracing their social history. Thus religion is criticized as an ideology. To show that God does not exist is as hopeless a venture as proving that he does exist. Instead, Marxism undertakes to show under what social circumstances religion was bound to develop. By this it will establish its transient character, at least if it can be shown that the social conditions which produced religion are a passing phenomenon. Marx and Engels discussed this point as follows: "When Feuerbach posited the religious world as the illusion of the . . . earthly world, another question, which he did not answer, came up automatically: Whence came it that men put these illusions into their own heads? And even for the German theoreticians this question opened the way toward a materialistic . . . and therefore for the first time *really* critical view of the world." [49] Several years earlier, Marx had already answered the question which Feuerbach had left unanswered. He had analyzed religion as the ideology of helplessness, misery, and despair, the call for help on the part of men who have not learned to help themselves.

The *misery* of *religion* is at once an *expression* of actual misery and also a *protestation* against actual misery. Religion is the sigh of the harassed creature, the heart of a heartless world, as it is the spirit of spiritless circumstances. It is the *opiate* of the people. . . . Religion is only the illusory sun which moves around man as long as man does not move around himself.[50]

Marxist writings often take the form of book reviews. Opposing ideologies are criticized, and then an attempt is made to analyze the relationship and institutions which led to the reign of this false consciousness. The criticism of ideas is thus inseparable from a criticism of society. In attacking either, the Marxist, by implication at least, inevitably attacks the other. Hence Marx could write, "The abolition of religion, being the illusory happiness of the people, is a demand for their real happiness. The demand that one reject illusions about one's situation is a demand that one reject a situation which has need for illusion." And further: "Criticism of heaven thus is transformed into a criticism of the earth, *criticism of religion* into the *criticism of the law, criticism of theology* into the *criticism of politics*." [51]

In all its aspects and ramifications, the concept of alienation makes us aware of the close unity of Marxist analysis and Marxist criticism. As has been pointed out, Marxist sociology is greatly indebted to the thought of German romanticism and its critique of modern civilization. Like the romantics, Marx posits a noble and intelligent human species, the potentialities of which are frustrated in their development by the ills of civilization. Human relationships are utilitarian and exploitative; but they are so not because of any inherent human nature, as the utilitarians would maintain, but because the given class structure compels individuals and groups to act only according to narrow self-interest. As the superstructure acquires more and more independence, that of the individual is lessened, with the result that, with the division of labor, the primary social relations which are behind the superstructure are obscured and man's intelligence becomes frustrated.

The resulting image of man and what he has made of himself is gloomy and pessimistic. In his attempt to master the forces of nature, man has created social relationships and institutions which have become a tyrannic and frustrating second nature. His physical, emotional, and intellectual potentialities have been stunted. He has been rendered helpless, vicious, and blind. In this theory of alienation, man's aim to produce the necessities of life plays a role somewhat analogous to the Original Sin of Christian mythology. And from the theory we have presented so far it might seem that Marx and Engels despair of man's redemption from the state of alienation.

This is, of course, only a partial view of Marxist theory. The gloomy image of man's alienation is matched by the hopeful prospect of a bright future, a future which is seen to be within close reach. It is this optimistic prognosis contained in Marxist theory with which we shall deal now.

Chapter Three

The Faith in Progress

Hegel designates the role of evil in world history as a positive one. By the "cunning of reason" which is immanent in all things, evil does pioneer work for the Good by sharpening antagonisms, causing them to clash with each other, and finally reconciling them in a higher unity.   Joachim Schumacher

Modern Industry . . . compels society, under penalty of death, to replace the detail-worker of to-day, crippled by life-long repetition of one and the same trivial operation, and thus reduced to the mere fragment of a man, by the fully developed individual, fit for a variety of labours, ready to face any change of production, and to whom the different social functions he performs, are but so many modes of giving free scope to his own natural and acquired powers.   Karl Marx

The Promethean Image of Man

Marxism has its deep roots in the Western humanist tradition; and the biases and values of this tradition are injected into the Marxist image of society, its origins, and its ills. But this humanism is contained in Marxist theory in different and quite contradictory forms. One of the strands that has been picked up from the web of humanist value judgments and preconceptions is an idealized image of natural man unspoiled by civilization, an idea of an altruistic, coöperative, kind, social animal with a childlike, sunny disposition. This is, basically, the romantic image of human nature, which carries with it a great attachment to aesthetic and emotional values, a glorification of the beauties and virtues inherent in natural things and natural relationships. Like the romantics, Marx profoundly deplores the fact that civilization has alienated this natural man from his natural environment and from his own good nature. From the preceding chapter we have seen that he has been spoiled, seemingly beyond redemption.

But Marx was not a romantic. He did not lose himself in wishdreams about returning to a golden age of the past. He was not only a critic, but had definite ideas about a future good society which would be far more desirable than the age of primitive tribal communism. And this concept of the future is connected with an entirely different image of human nature, a different set of preconceptions and values. From the same broad humanist tradition Marx has appropriated for his system a Promethean image of man the creator, man the provider, man the tamer of his environment. He has identified himself with a glorification of material achievements which, before him, had been an essential part of revolutionary liberalism, part of the ideology of the rising bourgeoisie. The labor theory of value, which Marx took over from the classical economists of free enterprise, is an outstanding symbol of this Promethean image of man. It is from this heritage that Marx derived his interpretation of history as a process of change in the method by which men attempt to master the forces of nature, as the evolution of modes of production, and as the creation of ever more complex and rational systems of social organization. As Prometheus seized the heavenly fire to make life more livable on earth, so man has made the earth a place on which to live more easily, more comfortably, more securely. Man himself has grown in stature through this process. He has acquired amazing strength and awe-inspiring knowledge. The fire of Prometheus has not only warmed his hut, it has also dispelled the night before his eyes.

The Marxist insistence on materialism in social science symbolizes these ideas: it says that the world is objective reality which lies ready to be grasped and mastered by the cognitive minds and the purposive hands of men. This materialistic faith — or, as we have called it, this realism — is bluntly directed against those schools of philosophy which deny or doubt the objective reality of the outside world or claim that man can never acquire full knowledge of it. It attacks subjectivist schools of epistemology whose point of departure is man's mind, so that the outside world turns into a derivative, as it were, of our senses.[1]

Whether we call it materialism or realism, this assertion that the world exists objectively is, in the last analysis, no more than a faith. Attempts to refute the claims of idealism and subjectivism rest either on circular reasoning or on silent assumptions which, when examined, leave the dispute unresolved. Someone tells of Lenin trying, in a heated argument, to prove the correctness of this materialism to a neo-Kantian opponent; he is said to have battered his fist against a wall and to have cried, "Look at this stone wall! You see it, you can feel it, and here I am knocking my hand bloody against it. And you want to deny or doubt its objective reality?" Philosophically, Lenin's argument begged the question.[2] Yet, the fact that we can all repeat this act, the fact that we all shall bloody our fists if we knock them against brick walls, is a cogent argument for the adoption of the materialist faith as a working hypothesis. Whatever the philosophical inadequacies of this position, it is no more than good common sense to assume the material reality of things against which we constantly knock ourselves sore. Just as the refinements of the modern theories of indeterminacy and relativity do not affect the validity of fundamental mechanical laws while we are dealing with common-sense magnitudes, so some of the refinements of philosophy are wasted on the social scientist. The philosophical error of Marxism does not consist in accepting the materialist hypothesis, but in accepting this common-sense notion dogmatically, unquestioningly, and without qualifications. Or, we might say, the error of Marx's followers consists in elevating Marx's common sense into a philosophical statement.

A close connection exists between materialism, radicalism, and optimism. Why does Marxism insist so determinedly on the materialist dogma? For one thing, it is because its founders were critical of the environment; and this critical attitude created in them an insatiable craving for knowledge of this world against which they assert we knock ourselves bloody. The criticism of Marx and Engels is directed toward the outside, against the en-

vironment, and not toward our own frailties and failures. In the
joint work which summarizes their early philosophical views
they wrote: "Dissatisfaction with oneself is either dissatisfaction
with oneself within a certain environment conditioning the entire personality (e.g., dissatisfaction with oneself as a worker)
— or moral dissatisfaction. In the first case it is thus simultaneously and primarily dissatisfaction with the existing conditions;
in the second case it is an ideological expression of these conditions themselves, which in no ways transcends them, but is
part of them." [3] In short, they claim that criticism will be effective only as long as it is based on a materialist analysis of the
outside world. Thus, even if the connection between materialism and radicalism may not be logically necessary, as Marxists
tend to claim, there is a decided pragmatic tie. Marx and Engels
pleaded for materialism on the ground that only a realistic
analyst of the social system can be an effective and successful
radical. Only a realist, too, can hope to act rationally upon his
environment. The materialist faith that the world is real is thus
an essential part of the Promethean image of man, a man who
recognizes obstacles, removes them, and creates improvements.

We must realize the force of these humanist preconceptions
in Marxist theory in order to understand the revulsion and in-
dignation which any type of Malthusian theory evokes in every
Marxist.[4] "The highest being for man is man himself," so that
even a resigned justification of human misery runs counter to
the very basis of Marxist theory. The implicit assumption is
also that man will succeed in making nature yield abundantly
the means of life. To doubt this ability to produce abundance,
to doubt that the earth is big enough for its population, is re-
pugnant to the humanist with his exalted Promethean conception of man.[5] And similar repugnance meets any other theory
which doubts man's ability to master his environment or to gain
full knowledge of the world.

This view of human nature serves as the indispensable basis
for all the sanguine optimism which Marxist theory breathes.
We shall see that it underlies Marx's expectancy of a proletarian
revolution, though we shall have to examine whether this optimistic prognosis is not belied by the entire theory of alienation.

And we shall further recognize that the image of socialism presupposes the Promethean conception of man and rests on the glorification of material achievement. It is to this image of socialist society that we now turn our attention.

Socialism — A Society Worthy of Man

Marxism claims that it has uncovered in bourgeois society not only elements of disintegration which spell its approaching doom, but also constructive features that provide hope for a better future. From the theory of surplus value, Marx derived three basic laws. First, according to the law of capitalist accumulation, competition forces the capitalist to accumulate capital in order to save labor. But by increasing the proportion of machinery to labor, the capitalist causes a fall in his profits, dependent as they are on the use of wage labor. Second, the law of the concentration of capital asserts that competition drives the weaker capitalists from the field, thus swelling the ranks of free labor, while concentrating capital in the hands of fewer and fewer capitalists, who gradually turn into monopolists. Last, the law of increasing misery holds that the capitalist, forced to compensate for the decline in his profits, must intensify his exploitation of the workers by extorting more and more surplus labor from them. Growing unemployment meanwhile creates an industrial reserve army, forcing the worker into accepting any conditions laid down by the capitalist. Hence the more capital is in circulation, the greater will be the production output, but the less will be the labor employed and the wages it receives. The accumulation of wealth in capitalist society is accompanied by the increasing misery of the broad masses of the population, or, as Marx called it, the "accumulation of misery, agony of toil, slavery, ignorance, brutality, mental degradation. . . ." [6] Hundreds of pages in the writings of Marx and Engels are filled with eloquent and wrathful descriptions of the unspeakable social consequences of capitalism, that mode of production in which man is made into a commodity and becomes an adjunct of a machine which sucks him dry of his very life. Marx and Engels have convincingly shown that the working class in the early decades of capitalism lived a life more miserable

than that of draft animals. They have demonstrated the limitless-
ness of degradation and despair, of moral, physical, and intellectual destruction which this existence brought with it. No one
can read these well-documented descriptions of proletarian life
in the Victorian age without a shudder of incredulity, revulsion,
and pity.

The ultimate results of these "historical tendencies of capitalist
accumulation" are spelled out by Marx in the following words:
"Along with the constantly diminishing number of the magnates
of capital who usurp and monopolize all advantages of this
process of transformation grows the mass of misery, oppression,
slavery, degradation, exploitation; but with this too grows the
revolt of the working class, a class always increasing in numbers,
and disciplined, united, organized by the very mechanism of
the process of capitalist production itself. The monopoly of capital becomes a fetter upon the mode of production which has
sprung up and flourished along with and under it. Centralization
of the means of production and socialization of labor at last
reach a point where they become incompatible with their capitalist integument. This integument is burst asunder. The knell of
capitalist private property sounds. The expropriators are expropriated." [7]

Analyzing capitalism in purely economic terms (though stressing the consequences of this system for the human beings that
live under its sway), Marx has drawn a picture of an economic
system racked by ever-recurring crises, each more disastrous than
the preceding one. These crises are the result of intrinsically
irreconcilable features inherent in the system, features which
can be removed only by force. This force is exerted in the class
struggle. As we have pointed out, Marx is careful to explain
that, in the struggle between capital and labor over the length of
the working day, both are only maintaining their rights as pur-
chasers or sellers of labor power. Hence, concludes Marx, "there
is here . . . an antinomy, right against right, both equally
bearing the seal of the law of exchanges. *Between equal rights
force decides.* Hence it is that in the history of capitalist production, the determination of what is a working day, presents
itself as the result of a struggle between collective capital, i.e.,

the class of capitalists, and collective labour, i.e., the working class." [8]

The end of this mode of production approaches when the final crisis sets in; and here too, in describing this last crisis of capitalism, Marx abandons economic terminology and begins to speak of a political event, the proletarian revolution. Neither he nor Engels were very specific in outlining the features and consequences of this revolution. Essentially, they thought of it as a brief period of political violence in the course of which power is seized by the industrial proletariat, followed by a thorough transformation of the economic relationships when the owners of productive capital are expropriated. The industrial establishment and all other means of production and communication are taken over by the great majority of society in the name of everyone, collectively. Society as a whole will take charge of the productive process. In this sense, the dictatorship of the proletariat will not mean that a new ruling class has taken over; on the contrary, the "working class . . . will substitute for the old civil society an association which will exclude classes and their antagonism." [9] "When the proletariat triumphs, it then by no means becomes the absolute side of society, since it triumphs only in that it annihilates itself and its opposite. The proletariat itself disappears no less than its conditioning opposite, private property." [10] "The condition for the emancipation of the working class is the abolition of every class, just as the condition for the liberation of the Third Estate — of the bourgeois order — was the abolition of all estates and all orders." [11]

This reasoning is unassailable only because it is circular. It is a matter of definition that everyone's property is no one's property and that a society in which everyone is a proletarian is a classless society, in the sense that there are no class differences. Nor is it difficult to understand why Marx could claim that the proletariat abolishes itself by abolishing class differences, since the very term "proletariat" is a term of class differentiation. Here too the argument is nothing more than the juggling of definitions.

Marx's confidence that no new ruling class need arise, once property has been appropriated in the name of society by the proletariat, rests on his belief that all divisions of labor could be abolished in the postcapitalist society. He held that under capitalism the production process had been so rationalized and concentrated that it could be centrally planned and directed, and the entrepreneur had become superfluous. Moreover, the last progressive function of the superfluous class, the bourgeoisie, had been to train its successor, the proletariat, by arming and equipping it for modern production. The bourgeoisie, in short, had made it possible for the working class to take over. The struggle which the workers were waging, spontaneously, against capitalism had turned them into a political force; the economic struggle of isolated individuals had turned into the political struggle of a class.[12] And this fact of its being organized as a class for political struggle meant, to Marx, that the proletariat was now ready to rule. "An oppressed class," he wrote in 1846, "is the vital condition for every society founded on the antagonism of classes. The emancipation of the oppressed class thus implies necessarily the creation of a new society. For the oppressed class to be able to emancipate itself it is necessary that the productive powers already acquired and the existing social relations should no longer be capable of existing side by side. Of all the instruments of production, the greatest productive power is the revolutionary class itself. The organization of revolutionary elements as a class supposes the existence of all the productive forces which could be engendered in the bosom of the old society." [13]

But this was not all. The expropriation of the capitalists would not mean the ascent of another ruling class. In the Marxist view, the modern machine had so leveled productive skills that no more specialization was necessary, and the entrepreneur had become superfluous, anyway, being seen merely as the provider of capital. "Only now . . . has any ruling and exploiting class become superfluous, nay, an obstacle to social development." [14] Marx and Engels thus had an idealized and quite premature conception of modern industrial society as a push-button shop, without realizing the complex technical demands such a society would make.

Given these premises (the abolition of private property in the means of production and the obsolescence of the division of labor), socialism would mean the abolition of commodity production. In other words, lacking the necessity for profits to keep plants in operation, production would be for use, and no longer for the market. "In a future society, in which class antagonisms will have ceased, in which there will no longer be any classes, use will no longer be determined by the minimum time of production [that is, people will no longer be forced to buy the cheapest and poorest products] but the time of production devoted to an article will be determined by the degree of its utility [that is, the needs of society will determine what is to be produced]." [15] As the Communist Manifesto expresses it: "In bourgeois society living labor is only a means by which to increase accumulated labor. In communist society accumulated labor is but a means by which to broaden, enrich, and further the workers' life process. Hence in bourgeois society the past rules over the present, in communist society the present over the past." In bourgeois society, individuals and classes are under the domination of the machine and the social system created by previous generations; in the socialist society envisaged by Marxism, social institutions and the machinery of production would be in the service of mankind.

All this rests on one further premise, the production of abundance. Marx and Engels firmly believed that all necessary preconditions had been created for producing abundantly. With the greatest heat they lashed out against the gloomy analysis of Malthus and asserted that there were absolutely no limits to capitalist production, except the social relations of capitalism themselves. If the existing social order which perpetuates commodity production were smashed, then the road to the production abundance would be open. "That is today no longer a fantasy, a pious wish. With the present development of productive forces, that increase in production will suffice which is given by the fact of the socialization of the means of production alone." [16]

The expropriation of the expropriators would thus free mankind from material needs. Only then would man be able for the first time to pursue politics, religion, science, art, and other interests. Alienation would be abolished in all its features. There would be no more suppression and exploitation of man by man. The abolition of commodity production would mean the restoration of individual property in the Lockian sense as "that property which men have in their persons as well as goods." [17] Finally, the entire superstructure, which is, after all, only a product of class antagonism, would wither away. The state would dry up, as it were, since there would be no more class struggles that might express themselves in a political power struggle. In place of the state there would grow up a collectivist *Gemeinwesen* or community, administering the needs of all for the benefit of all, and with all participating. Law would wither away because the elimination of the class struggle would do away with the major conditions making for crime and litigation. Man's various social functions, like propagation and education, would burst out of the reified shell in which class society had imprisoned them and would become spontaneous and unconstrained. Ideology, as false consciousness, would be supplanted by true consciousness, expressing man's mastery over nature, society, and himself. Art and other forms of play would be liberated from their determination by the class struggle and would therefore be free to develop spontaneously all the potentialities inherent in them. Even morality could now blossom forth, a "truly human ethic, standing above class contradictions and above the memory of them." [18] For the first time men would be free to be truly human.

Dialectics — Science of Progress?

In asserting that their view of the socialist future was a scientific prognosis, not a utopia, Marx and Engels were really making two claims. First, they asserted that their program of action was based on a realistic (scientific) appraisal of the given situation. Second, they claimed that the vision of the future which they outlined in such optimistic tones was not a dream, but an equally realistic description of positive trends existing within the old social order. Scientific socialism — that meant the assertion that the coming of the socialist society was inevitable.

We have seen the reasons Marx and Engels advanced to substantiate this claim. In two ways, they thought, the working-out of the capitalist system has made the coming of socialism inevitable. For one thing, they concluded from their analysis that capitalism was doomed. Given the present social order, nothing but crises, depressions, ruinous wars, and general misery could be expected. But this crisis of capitalism would not lead to the disintegration of our civilization. For a constructive force had been created within the womb of the old order: the industrial working class, rising to emancipate itself from exploitation, would emancipate the entire society from the fetters of capitalist relationships.

We shall have to pay very close attention to this second argument, because it comes into conflict with the theory of alienation. The question to be asked is: how can the industrial working class, being so thoroughly alienated from its own human nature, have it within itself to achieve its own emancipation? We shall see in Chapter 4 how Marx answers this question. Before developing the Marxist image of the proletariat in detail, however, we shall have to investigate a more abstract aspect of the Marxist theory of progress, namely the Marxist belief, sometimes openly expressed, sometimes left implicit, that human progress in general is inevitable, that there are no insoluble problems for mankind.

Marx and Engels viewed history from the peak of modern industrial society and, following a deeply ingrained tradition of Western historiography, pressed all history into the mould of European development. With the hindsight of those who have reached spectacular heights, they considered all periods of past history as steps on the road to this pinnacle. History, for them, was the history of Western civilization, not the history of cultures as outlined by Vico, Herder, Danilevsky, Spengler, or Toynbee.

From the very beginning, therefore, Marx and Engels were trapped in the same fallacy which characterizes the theory of evolution. Both Marxism and Darwinism are preoccupied with success and progress, and with the way in which it has been achieved. Both schools tend to overlook the frequency of failure and the countless dead-end roads that have been taken both in history and in the evolution of species. Both tended to take the ultimate inevitability of progress for granted.

There is a close connection between this belief in inevitable progress and the functional view of reality. We have seen that this view is inherently teleological: society is seen as a "going concern"; it is seen as having a certain central air or purpose. If it goes no further than that, this sort of teleology might be entirely justified from the point of view of social science. After all, society is made up of human beings, and it is perfectly proper to attribute to human beings, either individually or in groups, certain basic aims, purposes, and drives, which find their outlet in all types of society.

Nor is it objectionable, as we have seen, to establish correspondences between various aspects of society, so that all parts of the whole are seen in functional relationship. If the central aim of mankind be the production of the means of life, then it is only logical to regard all human activities, institutions, and ideas in their relationship to the process of production. But Marx, Engels, and their followers have shown a persistent tendency to go further than that in several respects. First of all, they have time and again implied or stated that the emergence of functional features is inevitable. Though the class structure does not change in step with the development of technology, it will inevitably catch up. Though the superstructure lags behind the development of the forces in production, a functional superstructure is bound to be created in the end. This is, in short, the idea which was so widespread in the nineteenth century, that every society has that type of government it deserves; or that, if Napoleon had not been born, someone else would have played his role in a very similar manner.

Closely connected with this is Marx's conviction that the opposite of lag, the premature development of social relationships or superstructural institutions, is entirely impossible. "A social formation," he wrote, "never goes down until all those productive forces have been developed which it can embrace; and new, higher relations of production never come forth before the material conditions for their existence have been hatched in the loins of the old society itself. For this reason mankind never poses itself any tasks but those it knows how to solve." [19] In a similar vein, the young Marx had implied that the very recognition of a problem means it is going to be solved. "It will become apparent," he had written, "that mankind has long had the dream of a thing, of which it need only gain consciousness in order really to possess it." In both quotations the implication is that the very emergence of conscious ideas or of new social relationships is a sure indication that they are functional, that is, that they correspond to new forces of production that have been hatched in the womb of the old society.

But what about lag? Is it not a feature of disharmony and disfunction, and does it not impede the development of the forces of production? The Marxist reply would be that the forces of progress will, in the end, be bound to win out over all factors impeding their development. In the Marxist view, history does not stand for too intense a lag, and there is an inherent urge for functional harmony. New forces of production will conquer all obstacles presented by the old relations of production, and by the superstructure. Economic progress cannot be held back. No class can forever remain in power by methods which restrict or retard economic progress. As Lenin put it in a famous speech: "One can apply coercion without having economic roots, but in that case it is historically doomed to failure. But one can apply coercion basing oneself on the class of progress . . . *and then it can suffer a setback temporarily, but it cannot be licked.*" [20]

But every time the forces of progress have overcome the forces of reaction, lag is bound to set in. Each reintegration of society is followed by inevitable disintegration. All syntheses are ephemeral; things cannot stand still. "History as little as knowledge can find a final end in a perfect, ideal state of mankind; a perfect society, a perfect 'state,' are things that can exist only in fantasy." [21] Moreover, the forces of production themselves, prime movers of progress in the Marxist view, do not develop independently from the social development as a whole; nothing in Marxism suggests that there is any independent life in technological progress as such. Nor is the development of the economic substructure seen as a cause, and superstructural phenomena as effects. No, the development of the substructure is as much effect as cause of the superstructure. Indeed, we might even go so far as to say that it is lag, more than anything else, which stimulates the development of the forces of production. Just because there are forces of stagnation and disharmony, new, progressive forces develop which will be able to overcome the insoluble dilemmas of the old society. There is progress just because there is lag; integration, just because there is disintegration.[22]

Many Marxists have buttressed this belief in the inevitability of progress — and it is no more than a belief — by the laws, so-called, of dialectics. Dialectics thus is seen as a theory of emergence of creation; and this theory is phrased in a number of different ways. There is, first of all, the image of the unity and struggle of opposites: opposites clash. In clashing, each affects the other and in turn changes its own nature, and, in the end, both emerge out of the struggle as a different object. The conflict has been resolved by the elimination of the antagonistic units, and all subsequent conflict is a conflict between new opposites, hence a conflict on a different and, presumably, higher plane. Both thesis and antithesis are eliminated by the synthesis. Yet, why the struggle of opposites should always, or ever, be resolved by a synthesis is not at all explained. Nor does this theory make clear why the resolution of such a clash must necessarily be a step in the right direction. And we have not even made mention of the essential meaninglessness of every single concept used in this image of the "unity and struggle of opposites."

Another way by which to make dialectics into a theory of creation is to dwell on the emergence of new qualities, and to differentiate qualitative from quantitative change.[23] We must again question the assumption that the emergence of a new quality, so-called, is inevitably a progressive step. This, however, is the very definite implication, an implication which is spelled out by the use of the word *aufheben* when speaking of the dialectical triad — this German verb with its triple meaning of eliminating, lifting up, and preserving. The example which Engels gives in his polemic against Dühring illustrates the belief in progress which the concept of the double negation implies. Engels speaks of the barley plant.[24] The seed, he says, is the thesis; the plant into which the grain develops (in proper soil and under proper conditions) is its negation; and the ear bearing its multitude of new barley grains is the negation of the negation. After the ear develops, both seed and plant die — thesis and antithesis are eliminated. But the ear is at the same time the original grain lifted onto a higher plane — because it has been multiplied. In the ear, the seed has been *aufgehoben*.

The necessity for proper soil and proper conditions to make the negation possible cannot be overstressed, and it points to the inadequacy of the term itself. Negation, as used by the Marxists, does not mean destruction and annihilation, though a certain amount of destruction goes with it. But the word *aufheben* constitutes a warning that negation must be constructive. The forces of rebellion must destroy only what is obsolete and preserve all that has meaning and value. Only thus will the entire organism be lifted onto a higher plane. All progress toward a desirable goal means not only negation but also, simultaneously, preservation. Negation must permit reinstitution, and the foe of the old order must be discriminating in his negative, destructive efforts. "Each kind of thing," wrote Engels, "has . . . its own characteristic manner so to be negated that the result is development, so also each kind of ideas and concepts." [25] And Lenin, in the same vein, admonished: "Not naked negation, not blind negation . . . are characteristic of, and essential to, dialectics — which doubtless contains an element of negation, and even as its most important element — no, but negation as a 'moment' of connection, as a 'moment' of development, with the conservation of all that is positive . . ." [26] Similarly, Engels pointed out that burning a grain does not negate it; to be negated it has to be planted in the soil. And Lenin again put the same thought picturesquely by writing: "Destroyed capitalism won't fill your stomachs. You have," he added, "to seize the entire culture which capitalism has left, and, out of it, construct socialism." [27]

These admonitions are very sensible indeed. But they also create bewilderment. For dialectics furnishes no criteria whatever to distinguish a correct negation from an incorrect one.

And even if such a criterion were furnished by Marxist theory, we should once again have to ask for proof that this kind of correct negation is inevitably bound to be made. What guarantee is there that the progressive solution is always, or ever, found? Dialectics gives not the slightest indication of an answer to this. It may be an interesting and suggestive way of formulating the morphology of change and even of progress, but it can in no wise serve as a demonstration that progress is inevitable. Nevertheless, the slipperiness of its terminology has led many Marxists and non-Marxists to use it for attempts to establish just such proof. Purpose and aim have been read into history, and dialectical laws have been adduced in support of such views. In this way it has been converted into some sort of animistic religion, or into some sort of conceptual hocus-pocus which could be used to prove literally everything.

Dialectics has therefore become the major source of embarrassment for many writers who called themselves Marxists or sought to defend Marxist theories. To appreciate the dilemma into which those, who endeavor to defend the commonly accepted interpretation of dialectics without transcending the bounds of common sense, place themselves one ought, perhaps, to read the pertinent chapter in G. D. H. Cole's *What Marx Really Meant*, and particularly the desperate last sentences in which the blame is placed on the reader in the event that he has not understood the author's tortuous discussions. The title of Cole's book is significant. It indicates that the Marxist terms are esoteric and bewildering. Taken at face value, they are philosophically indefensible and violate common sense, to boot. If the Marxist system is to be preserved, dialectics has either to be explained as we have attempted in the foregoing pages, or abandoned entirely. And the idea which calls for the greatest amount of explanation is the concept of inevitable progress. One school, the so-called revisionists, turn inevitability into moral necessity. Adherents to a more orthodox letter of Marxist thought, on the other hand, have tended to dilute it into meaning no more than the possibility of progress.

Yet Marx and Engels did not say "possibility"; again and again they used the word "inevitability" or the word "necessity." Nor could the latter term have had an exclusively moral connotation.

Necessity, in Marxist writings, means both moral necessity and empirically observable inevitable trend. Marx and Engels were demonstrably convinced that they had found scientific evidence for the existence of aim and purpose in historical development. The teleological aspects of history could be demonstrated, they thought. But the reason was neither a mysterious dialectical force nor moral necessity. The mainspring of progress, in Marxist dialectics, can only be sought in the Marxist idea of human nature: *if lag leads to progress, if the dead weight of superannuated institutions gives a stimulus to the development of the forces of production, it can only be because man will not tolerate stagnation or retrogression. The development of new and better productive forces, and progress itself, is not something autonomous; it is the product of men. And lag leads to progress precisely when it becomes excessive, because then it dramatizes the need for progress and, by creating particular grievances, points the way toward their relief. Lag produces progress because it is a stimulus for remedial action.*

For man, according to the dictum of Engels, is a conscious and purposive animal; and anything in Marxism that smacks of determinism, destiny, or teleology, is explained by the assumption that history is made by man. So that we can restate the Marxian creed by saying that not economics, but intelligent action will ultimately triumph over the forces which have so far determined man and society.

At this point the reader may recall the Marxist theory of alienation, and realize that it is in fundamental conflict with what has just been stated. The development of civilization, according to this theory, had brought about the alienation of man from his natural environment and his natural gifts. His bonds with nature had been torn; his inborn intelligence had been frustrated. Hence, if the Marxist theory of progress rests on the assumption that man is an intelligent animal, would we not have to conclude that the preconditions of further progress have disappeared? Let us see, in the next chapter, how Marx answers this question. The essence of this answer, we shall see, consists of a very special view of the proletariat, its nature, and the role it is destined to play.

Chapter Four

The Unity of Theory
and Practice

*. . . For the change in human nature which produces Communist
consciousness on a mass scale can occur only in the practical activity of making revolution.*

Karl Marx and Friedrich Engels

We have listened to Marx's indictment of capitalism and have
sketched his view of a future more worthy of man's dignity and
potentialities. Though in his criticism he was following in the
footsteps of romanticism, Marx was by no means a romantic.
He did not wish to return from the evil bourgeois age to some
medieval, Christian, or classical ideal; on the contrary, the societies that have preceded capitalism are in many ways subjected
to even sharper criticism, so that, in terms of what has preceded
it, capitalism is considered progressive, and the bourgeois revolution, the most important milestone in man's road to freedom.
For it has opened an era in which a productive system could be
built up which, in the Marxist view, has taken mankind to the
threshold of its final liberation. Thus the Marxist attitude toward capitalism, as indeed toward everything that exists, is
starkly ambivalent, and, in that sense, far more sophisticated than
merely apologetic or condemnatory.

This is reflected in the Marxist program designed to abolish
capitalism and its ills. The romantic critics of bourgeois society
had advocated a number of ways by which the individual could
overcome the evils of modern civilization. But all these ways —
whether they involved emulation of the simple folk in backward

or rural areas, a turning again to the bliss of an allegedly un-tarnished past, a return to a truly religious spirit, a preoccupation with philosophic speculation, or the contemplation of the beauti-ful — were open only to a very few individuals, mostly edu-cated people with sufficient means. In the Marxist view, there-fore, they were nothing more than highly illusory escapes from the real problems which would continue to exist; they amounted to the individual creation of a dream world which left the ugly reality of the modern world intact. Against this, Marx builds his prognosis for a better future on all that exists. The capitalist system, with all its abominations, contains the promise of a Good Society; and, even though, like Moses, the bourgeois order itself is unable to cross into the promised land, it does at least provide the vista.

Marxist radicalism is made up of these two midnineteenth-century clichés: that the existing social structure and institutions, by-products of man's material achievements, are unworthy of his natural dignity, and that man's inherent potentialities are manifested in his material achievements and his rational, con-scious organization. Contradictory as these two attitudes seem to be, Marxism resolves the seeming contradiction and recon-ciles the two value systems by an ingenious proposition. Carried to its logical conclusion, material progress, formerly the source of man's alienation from his human qualities, will liberate him from the evils of civilization. Instead of alienating him from his inherent natural virtues, it will, instead, bring them out. The fullest possible development of his material achievement will enable man to be, for the first time, really himself. Having subdued the forces of nature, so that they will abundantly provide for his life, he will, under socialism, master also the social forces his ancestors have created. He will substitute con-scious and purposive history-making for the former process by which he was making history under the unknown compulsion of forces beyond his control. Only then will a truly human history begin.

Is this vision utopian? One feature which tends to support such a view has already been mentioned in passing; it is the naïve, idealized conception of modern industrial society as a type of social organization requiring neither specialized functions nor hierarchical relationships. Certainly the development of the social structure in the most industrialized countries of the world has not confirmed this notion. Nor were Marx and Engels justified in assuming that the changes in human nature produced by the abolition of classes and of the superstructure would take place at once, if at all.

But, even if we assumed that ideologies and the entire superstructure would wither away after the abolition of classes, was this decisive result as certain as Marx and Engels supposed? We might agree that certain contradictions, certain tendencies toward disintegration and crisis within the social and economic structure have arisen; also that the proletariat has developed as a distinct class in modern society, trained to read, run machines, and fight with up-to-date weapons. Granted these conditions, nevertheless, how could Marx and Engels be so sure that the proletariat would really act to destroy the old social system and usher in a socialist commonwealth? *Did not their faith in the rationality of the working class contradict their theory of ideology*, according to which all men view society through the distorting spectacles of class interest, and the ideology of the ruling class is fostered on the helpless minds of the exploited? If this were applied to the proletariat, inspired intellectuals like Marx and Engels might preach and persuade, but they could never hope to convince the workers to follow them in action.

The Marxist reply to this challenge is a curious one. The proletariat, they say, whose interests Marxist theory is supposed to reflect, is not just another group or another class. It is a class the nature of which is unprecedented. By its position in the process of production, it is the complete expression and veritable incarnation of society. At the same time, and because of this, it is a society all by itself, as it were, outside of bourgeois society. Though only negatively so far, it is, in the eyes of Marxism, a counter-society to the existing order, and in this sense, it is not a particular group within the bourgeois system, but its total negation. Hence it has complete detachment.

Many thinkers, from Aristotle to our time, have maintained that scientific study at its best requires a maximum of detachment. Spinoza as well as Pareto stressed that the social scientist must step outside his own environment, at least with his mind, in order to have a vantage point from which to view the object of his enquiries. Practical attempts to achieve such detachment can take the form of retirement into an ivory tower of pure contemplation; this was apparently the highest way of life according to Aristotle. Or else a radical negation of the entire social structure as it exists at present must estrange the social scientist from his environment. In either case perfect detachment is achieved only in the illusion of the thinker concerned. At the same time few people are capable of achieving even this relative detachment from their environment; for both the ivory-tower philosopher and the radical dissenter require an unusual degree of independence. In order to continue existing in their estrangement, they have to have that freedom from cares and wants which only millionaires and ascetics possess. It helps, too, to be rootless, cosmopolitan, declassed, and without strong ties to family, friends, and others that might lay a burdensome claim on the thinker's energies and loyalty. Whatever the difficulties, however, detachment is implicitly recognized as an ideal prerequisite of true scholarship by many theoretical systems, including Marxism.[1]

But at the same time Marxism stresses the inevitability of involvement. On October 29, 1918, a leading member of the Socialist-Revolutionary Party of Russia, already outlawed by the Soviet government, published an open letter which *Pravda* reprinted three weeks later. The author, a certain Pitirim Alexandrovich Sorokin, was known not only as a young leader in his party, but also as a promising social scientist teaching at St. Petersburg University. In his letter of 1918 Sorokin declared that he was giving up his party affiliation and renouncing all political activity whatever. "The past year of revolution," he wrote, "has taught me one thing: Politicians can err; political activity can be socially useful but it can also be socially harmful. But work in the area of science and education is always useful and always necessary to a nation." Lenin was very much interested in this document and commented on it both in speech and in writing. One point he made was that a renunciation of political activity, a flight into seemingly neutral pursuits, is in itself a political act. Conversely, no seemingly nonpolitical activity is in actual fact neutral. There is no escape from political partisanship, and attempts at an "inner emigration" are futile.

In short, Lenin denounced the pseudo-detachment of philosophical or sociological contemplation, claiming that the ivorytower dweller does not recognize his own political attitude. "The modesty of the positivist or pragmatist, far from being praiseworthy, shows only that he is afraid of science, lest it lead him to radical conclusions." [2] Marxism stresses the unreality of contemplation; it sees the academician in all his remoteness from life and its problems, and believes that scholarship produced in ivied halls and musty stacks can add nothing significant to our knowledge of society. In this one point its theory of knowledge is akin to that of the pragmatists for whom practical involvement in affairs is an essential part of the process of cognition. The thinker has to be actually confronted by a given problem before he can recognize it.

As Marx and Engels saw it, the proletariat was more deeply and more significantly involved in the social system than any other class. To them, the proletariat was the actual producer of commodities in the modern machine industry, and it was the actual sufferer of all the vicissitudes of capitalism. At the same time, they regarded this involvement as something which places the proletariat completely outside society. Alienation, driven to its extremes, was seen to have turned into something quite different. The division of labor, they held, had been driven to such length that it had turned into the outright negation of all differences in labor because man in the modern machine shop had himself become a button-pushing automaton. The idiocy of craft specialization had given way to the soulless robot. Further, exploitation had, in their eyes, turned into complete dehumanization in capitalist society, where man himself had turned into a commodity. And so, Marx could write in all earnestness that the proletariat was not human any more; in his eyes therefore it epitomized the entire inhumanity of the capitalist system.

Capitalism was that mode of production in which the market did more than regulate the flow of commodities; the market had come to govern the relationships between individuals and classes as well. Man had turned into a commodity to be bought and sold on the open market. Torn from all primary ties and primary group loyalties, alienated from the family, the nation, the community, the land, and the craft, the proletarian could be conscious only of the fact that he was, actually, no more than a commodity. Hence, as Lukács has pointed out, the class consciousness which Marx and Engels attributed to the proletariat was the self-consciousness of man as a commodity. This means that Marx and Engels thought the proletariat, as a class, would gain insight into the innermost secret of capitalist relationships. Once the true nature of capitalism became clear, the proletariat would come to see the logical and obvious step to end its alienation: the abolition of commodity production as such, through the expropriation of the capitalists.

In this sense, the class consciousness of the proletariat could be seen as the ideology to end all ideologies. Epitomizing the unsurpassable inhumanity of the capitalist system, the proletariat, according to Marx, could uncover the real roots of inhumanity and exploitation in all social systems past and present and could thus speak for the tortured and oppressed human race as such. In the opinion of Marxism, the class consciousness of the proletariat thus turns into a broad and challenging humanism, and this humanism can for the first time be scientific and realistic. That is what Engels meant when he wrote that the proletariat had become the heir of classical philosophy: "Only within the working class the German knack for theory continues to exist unchanged. Here it cannot be eradicated. . . . The more recklessly and daringly science progresses, the more it is consonant with the interests and endeavors of the workers. . . . The German workers' movement is the heir of German classical philosophy." [3]

This is the keystone of the Marxist construction, and, again, it is formed from a contradiction. From the different elements of humanism which Marxism absorbed we obtain conflicting views concerning man's intelligence, man's rationality, man's ability to make history. The theory of alienation leads directly to the theory of ideology, according to which civilized man is encased in the narrow boxes created by the division of labor, shut off from reality, and hence unable to survey and cognize it. Once the development of civilization has been started, therefore, man's intelligence is stunted more and more hopelessly. On the other hand, there is the materialist faith, closely tied with the Promethean image of man, that the outside world is a real object, on which he can work and which he can recognize. There are no hidden secrets that will forever baffle us; potentially, at least, we can know everything. The contradiction between these two views about man's capability of attaining knowledge is resolved by a construction that reminds us of the Chosen People myth. In the proletariat, actual existence and real understanding, practice and theory, become one. The old wisdom of Socrates, that we cannot know the Good without acting according to its precepts, is here revived, and the spirit of almost boundless optimism, so characteristic of the early nineteenth century, becomes an essential element of the Marxist system.

Moreover, says Marx, as the working class begins to become truly conscious of itself and its environment, thought can now become truly realistic, so that idea and reality, theory and practice, converge not only within the proletariat but also within the intellectuals. For, as the proletarian revolution is approaching, socialist thought can at last find roots in actual social developments: "As history moves forward, and with it the struggle of the proletariat assumes clearer outlines, [the Socialists] no longer need to seek science in their minds; they have only to take note of what is happening before their eyes and to become the mouthpiece of this." [4] This is the meaning of the Marxist claim that their communism is not an ideal state conceived by philosophical speculation, but is the expression of a real movement of a class, and that its premises are really existing social conditions.

It is at this point that the working class, which has hitherto existed only *in itself*, turns into a class *for itself*, that is, a class truly conscious of its nature, its environment, its true interests. It will be the first class in history to acquire a scientific conception (class consciousness) of its place in history and society.

Hence this is the point at which all false ideologies will wither away. In his polemic against Dühring, Engels warned against all and any antireligious agitation on the part of the Marxist-socialist movement. Persecution of believers, he argued, would only create in them a martyr complex and would thus serve to prolong the reign of religiousness. Instead, he was confident that religion would die a natural death as soon as man had achieved complete mastery over his natural and social environment. As soon as man can help himself, he has no more spiritual need of the idea that there is a God who will help him. God will die when man need no more say that man proposes, but God disposes.[5] "Where could Vulcanus prevail against Robert & Co., Jupiter against the lightning rod, and Hermes against the *Crédit Mobilier?* All mythology conquers and rules and shapes the forces of nature in the imagination and through the imagination; it disappears therefore with our real mastery over them." [6]

Marxist writings are by no means clear concerning the precise point at which the proletariat will be driven by its class position to see the light of truth. The word of Engels, that the proletariat is the heir of classical philosophy, makes it seem that the working class is fully and truly conscious of its social situation and the roots thereof, even while the capitalist system is still exploiting it. But there are passages in the early writings of Marx and Engels indicating that the abolition of false consciousness — in the bourgeoisie as well as in the proletariat — was assured only by the abolition of classes. Thus only the proletarian revolution itself will give true consciousness to the working class and make it intellectually fit to run the affairs of society. "For the change in human nature which produces communist consciousness on a mass scale can occur only in the practical activity of making revolution." [7] In this sense, the proletarian revolution, abolishing classes and assuring man's mastery over himself and his social relations, would be truly philosophical achievement. The as yet unsolved problems of philosophy would be solved by a historical act. That is what Marx means when he says that action is necessary to liberate men's minds from the fetters of false consciousness.[8]

Moreover, theory itself assumes fundamental importance. We

have seen that one of the basic axioms of historical materialism was that ideas do not make history. But this does not mean they are ineffective. What it does mean is that ideas by themselves cannot make history. Yet, when they reflect actual social processes, they will be realized, and will even aid in the completion of the processes they reflect. "It is not sufficient that the idea strive toward its own realization, reality must itself strive toward the idea," the young Marx wrote; and, in the same work: "Theory is going to be realized among any nation only to such an extent as it means the realization of its needs." [9]

And how does theory aid in the completion of historical processes? By dramatizing them in the minds of men; by making men conscious of their own position, their own aspirations and interests. The modern proletariat may be driven to self-consciousness by the conditions into which the capitalist system has cast it. But both Marx and his twentieth-century communist followers believe that it takes a formulated and systematized theory to awaken the proletariat and convert its latent, spontaneous class-consciousness into a rational spur and guide to revolutionary action. "Criticism has plucked to pieces the imaginary flowers in the chain, not that man should bear the fanciless chain, the chain without consolation, but that he may throw off the chain, and break the living flower." [10]

A German Marxist has pointed out that Karl Marx did not "create the proletarian class movement. Nor did he create the class consciousness of the proletariat. But he did create the appropriate theoretically scientific expression for the new consciousness of the proletarian class, and with this, at the same time, lifted proletarian class consciousness onto a higher plane of existence. The transformation of the 'spontaneous' class views of the proletariat into theoretical concepts and theorems, and the mighty construction of the sysem of 'scientific socialism' out of all these theoretical laws, must not under any circumstances be viewed as a merely passive 'reflection' of the real historical movement of the proletariat. Instead, it forms an essential element of this real historical process itself. The historical movement of the proletariat could become neither 'independent' nor 'unified' without the formation of an independent and unified proletarian class consciousness." [11] This is more than the opinion of one individual Marxist scholar; it is the expression of an idea which forms part of the thought of both Marx and Lenin.

According to this view, therefore, irrational class interest has merged with true reason in the socialist movement. Communist theory reflects the class interest of the proletariat and contributes to awakening that class politically. At the same time the proletariat would not be receptive to this ideology if its own conditions did not serve as an uninterrupted lesson in the nature and origin of these conditions. Thought and reality, theory and practice, seem to have come together. The intellectual has found his way to the masses, and the masses can at last hope to speak the same language as the intellectual, as both the intellectual and the masses are driven to joint revolutionary action. Social science seems to have become popular and radical; radicalism appears to have become scientific; and a most novel theory of progress is the result.

PART II

THE DISINTEGRATION OF MARXISM

Chapter Five

Marxism as Ideology

It is with the mysteries of our religion, as with wholesome pills for the sick, which swallowed whole have the virtue to cure, but chewed are for the most part cast up again without effect.

Thomas Hobbes

The Disintegration of Marxism

The preceding chapters have explored the Marxist image of reality. On various levels of abstractness, we have traced Marx's preoccupation with human relationships, a preoccupation which he considered to be one of the essential aspects of his materialism. We saw how closely this materialism, in all its various aspects, was related to the attitude of radical criticism. Moreover, radical criticism and materialist social science merged with yet another strand, the optimistic belief in the inevitability of progress which gives all of Marxist sociology a teleological cast. It is important to note that this is only one of several possible manners in which to describe Marxism. We have not only stated the structure of its essential ideas and theorems; by describing it as an attitude (radicalism), a belief (optimism), and a self-imposed standard (science), we have in effect given a description, not of Marxism, but of the Marxist as an ideal type. But these psychological elements of the movement are intimately related to the ideas in themselves. And in essaying to trace the reasons for its disintegration, we have done less than half of the job if we merely criticize the validity of the ideas. We must, instead, realize that, in the ideal type we have constructed or reconstructed, all three aspects, radicalism, optimism, and social science, seek constantly to support each other, *and that the basic*

unity of this entire system lies in the conviction that they do so.
This acceptance of the unity of radicalism, optimism, and social
science is the ultimate and essential meaning of Marxist dialectics. As soon, therefore, as the attitude of criticism, a dispassionate analysis of reality, and the belief in progress become
irreconcilable with each other because they yield conflicting
results, the entire system disintegrates and must become distorted if anyone tries against all odds to restore its unity. The
attempt, against all better judgment, to incorporate and express
these three psychological elements with undiminished strength
makes the whole system of ideas self-contradictory.

The theory of Marx and Engels thus disintegrates under the
weight of two heavy burdens. One of these is the great number
of its *intellectual* problems, that is, the sketchiness of many of
its ideas, its inner conflicts, its obscurities, and contradictions.
In turn, these difficulties are related to the ideological problem
of Marxism: even if the crudities of Engels's philosophic views
or the inadequacies of Marx's economics could not destroy the
basic structure of the theory — and a case can be made for
this view — Marxism stands or falls with the unity of compat-
ibility of its three main psychological strands, radical criticism,
sober social science, and sure confidence in progress.

There is a link between the theoretical structure of Marxism
and the psychological functions it serves. This link is the doctrine of *the unity of theory and practice in the proletarian
movement.* As Marx gradually detached himself from Hegelian
philosophy, the relationship between theory and practice was
the focus of all arguments, even though, as we have seen, a clear
and unambiguous theory never fully emerged. The "materialist"
opposition to Hegel's "spiritualism" merely subsumed ideas
under the concept of matter, so that a dualistic view could still
hide under the cloak of materialism. Nor is it sufficient to point
out that, according to Marx, ideas were superstructural and could
never change the world, as he asserts so abundantly in *Die
Deutsche Ideologie.* In his second "Thesis on Feuerbach," he
still asks himself whether objective truth can be attributed to
man's ideas. His answer is that this is not a theoretical, but a
practical problem; for, "in his practice man must . . . demon-

strate the truth of his thought . . ." He is thus taking a pragmatic view of knowledge, in that the adequacy of our ideas can
be verified only by action. Side by side with this, however, he
never ceased to imply that thought itself is a material force;[1]
knowledge is power; consciousness is the specifically human
driving force of history. The truth gives strength to the forces
of progress and paralyzes the old ruling classes.[2] It frees the
slave and makes our dreams come true. So theory is practice par
excellence, just as practice is theory. Similarly, Marx repudiated
all notions of universal morality. Here, too, his stand seems to
be close to the pragmatic one: our aims must be derived from
reality, if socialism is to become scientific. "We do not want to
anticipate the world dogmatically, but want to find the new
world only in our criticism of the old one." [3] This position does
not take into account the problem, already alluded to, that no
moral conclusions can be drawn from a mere description of
reality, unless at least one moral premise be given. We cannot
criticize reality scientifically, we can criticize it only on the basis
of preconceptions as to what is to be approved and what is to
be condemned. Marx would brush this objection aside, however,
and would thereby imply that the moral preconceptions underlying his criticism are either common-sense notions and therefore unchallengeable, or, that they are the generally accepted
moral notions of the Western-Christian-Humanist tradition.
More specifically, he would identify himself as the spiritual
heir of the Jacobins, and claim that in his criticism of social reality
he was carrying on their revolutionary tradition. But once the
claim has been made that the value judgments of Marxism are
scientific, moralizing arguments are used with great abandon.
More than that, the doctrine of the unity of theory and practice
implies that even morality is a material force, an indispensable
element in revolutionary development.[4]

In short, the doctrine of the unity of theory and practice ob-
literates all differences between science and ethics, and tries to
unite both in an all-embracing world outlook, in which ethics is
derived scientifically, but social science is scientific only when it
is ethical. The doctrine thus springs from the radical revolutionary's yearning to fight for progress with open eyes, guided by

scientific knowledge about the world, and from his striving for reassurance that the god of history looks upon his efforts with favor. In turn, it helps to perpetuate the most conspicuous methodological fallacies which Marxism inherited from Hegel: if thought and reality are one, then the identity of logic and ontology, of epistemology and metaphysics, makes good sense; a monistic view of material processes, subsuming conscious human action under the concept of material reality, can finally lead to that animistic faith in progress in which purpose, cause, and function are virtually identified.

It is a commonplace observation that Marxism is a monistic view of history. The essence of this monism, however, is not the alleged reduction of all history to economic developments; it is, instead, the elimination of both (divine) spirit and (dead) matter in favor of a historiography which reduces all events to the sovereign actions of mankind while maintaining at the same time that man is not only the subject, but also the object of history who changes himself by changing his environment. The validity of such a man-centered interpretation of history is today acknowledged implicitly by most social scientists, and explicitly by many who in no way belong to the Marxist camp.[5] But Marxism, as we have seen, goes further in its attempts to eliminate all traces of dualism from social theory. It sees the proletarian revolution dissolve all distinctions between idea and reality, thought and action, value judgments and statements of fact. If the writer's brief remarks concerning this monism in the concluding chapter are correct, then it is precisely in this that Marxism not only goes further than the bourgeois social science of our day, but also must be said to have gone too far. We can say, with the knowledge of hindsight, that the glorious vision of Marx was no more than a utopian dream; and its collapse is the most fundamental cause of the breakdown and disintegration of Marxism.

For all appearance to the contrary, the unity of social science, radical criticism, and confidence in progress, breaks up when the empirical premises underlying the doctrine of the unity of theory and practice are destroyed. Monism is then replaced by dualism in all aspects of the theory. Science and value judgment go their independent way and yield contradictory results. Practice and theory, movement and aim, causality and free will are no longer in harmony.

As we have seen, the Marxist image of the proletariat as the chosen people, — utterly alienated, hence able to overcome its alienation, dehumanized, hence ready to carry the torch for humanity, bare of all ideology, hence equipped to recognize the very roots of man's troubles, cut off from all primary ties, hence ready to rise in revolt against the entire social order, disciplined by the modern method of collective production, hence pioneers of a collectivist community life, — this image of the proletariat was the precondition for the belief in the unity of theory and practice, of radicalism, optimism, and empiricism. *An uncompromisingly critical ideology, in order to call itself scientific or realistic, must have a firm mass basis,* and the goal must be within reach. Otherwise the theory disintegrates into independent and mutually exclusive interpretations basing themselves on selected parts of the whole. The history of the Marxist movement, therefore, is intimately related to the ebb and flow of revolutionary situations or mass movements of revolt. Whenever these have arisen and the leaders' hopes have been stirred, theory and practice, value judgments and sober analysis have come together, and Marxism has been reintegrated. Whenever the existing order has seemed to rally in new eras of stability, Marxism has decayed into a number of caricatures of the original ideology. In the following pages we shall trace the history of the movement up to World War I, from this point of view.

Marxism after 1848

Marxism before 1848 had little practical connection with a broad or significant political movement. Its followers were a tiny group of intellectuals and conspirators who, in turn, consorted with most of the other important conspiratorial circles of Western Europe. Yet Marx and Engels were convinced that a real mass movement existed side by side with their conspiratorial cell and that the aims and future actions of this mass movement were in conformity with their prognosis. The events of 1848 belied this conviction. After the big explosion in March, when all of Europe except England and Russia was rocked by radical upheavals, the revolution ebbed away. In every country compromises were found, and one radical fringe after the other was eliminated. Most disappointing for Marx and Engels was that there was *only a minimum of independent proletarian activity* except in Paris and Berlin. Altogether, few revolutions had been expected so openly and failed so miserably as that of 1848. The Marxist image of the proletariat had turned out to be a phantom.

The effect of this on Marxist theory has not been appreciated sufficiently, perhaps because it has been customary to consider the theories of Marx and Engels too much as a stable, unchanging ideology. To be sure, they themselves often implied that none of their basic ideas needed revision. But we need not take their word for this. Marx and Engels may have been insufficiently aware of the changes which the failure of 1848 had made necessary in their ideas and the problems that were created by these changes.

On the eve of the revolution, Marx, in his "Theses on Feuerbach," had bid goodbye to philosophy and intimated that revolutionary action was required to solve philosophical problems; and the Communist Manifesto had spelled out the nature and the consequences of this revolution. We have to be aware of this when we reread the manifesto today. The spectre of communism which Marx and Engels conjured up in their flaming pamphlet — a pamphlet in which all the ideas explained in the present work are presented in a nutshell — this spectre of communism was seen as a real and present threat to the existing order. The proletarian revolution was on the march. "Germany . . . is on the eve of a bourgeois revolution that is bound to be carried out under more advanced conditions of European civilization and with a much more developed proletariat than what existed in England in the 17th and in France in the 18th century . . ." For this reason, Marx and Engels believed that "the bourgeois revolution in Germany will be but the prelude to an immediately following proletarian revolution." [6]

This hope was disappointed, and soon afterwards Marx and Engels felt compelled to venture into very detailed analyses of political events and configurations in France, Germany, and England, with the aim of searching into the causes for the failure.

These political analyses are written in a tone of cocky assurance; one feels that the writers are satisfied with their method and feel, indeed, that the course of events has borne out their theories. Nonetheless we must realize that one of the motives for writing these articles, pamphlets, and monographs was an apologetic one: a momentous revolutionary upheaval, hailed in advance as the harbinger of a new and better society, had produced the regime of Napoleon III and strengthened reactionary dynasties everywhere. This called for explanations.

Of much greater importance for the development of Marxist ideology is the fact that this political stocktaking for the first time forced the founders of the movement to think extensively about problems of revolutionary strategy. Heretofore there had been an implicit faith in the spontaneous growth of the workers' movement, an implicit conviction that the proletariat would in fact rise and seize power into its hands. Now this belief gave room to the realization that the communist movement would have to work for the revolution, and that the problem of bringing it about speedily and effectively was by no means negligible. Hence the preoccupation with strategy, that is, with the when and where, the who and how of the proletarian revolution. Who, precisely, were the classes existing in contemporary society? What role did they play in furthering or obstructing the revolution? Where would the revolution come off first? How was its moment to be determined? And what action program should be evolved by the movement on the basis of such a diagnosis?

Maximum and Minimum Programs

One programmatic expression of the new preoccupation with revolutionary strategy is the increasing differentiation that came to be made between a maximum and a minimum program of the movement. This was made explicit in the program of the French Social-Democratic party which Marx dictated in 1880; but implicitly it pervades all the thinking that was done in the thirty preceding years. The minimum program was seen as a step toward the maximum aims. It consisted in the removal of all obstacles to the full flowering of capitalism and the pursuit of open class warfare. One major obstacle was presented by the prebourgeois classes that had managed to perpetuate themselves. These classes are neglected in the purley economic writings of Marx, where he discusses capitalism more abstractly as a pure system of only three classes, land owners, capitalists, and wage laborers. His political writings, on the other hand, single out the petty-bourgeoisie, an obsolete remnant of the past, as the chief frustrator of the revolution. Another essential element of the minimum program was the struggle for the extension of democratic liberties. From his observation of the events of 1848 Marx concluded that the bourgeoisie, heretofore the champion of democracy and civil rights, had become afraid of extending these rights; it was going back on those ideals with which it had been identified during its rise to power. Conversely, the political writings of Marx and Engels clearly imply that universal suffrage is a definite step toward proletarian revolution, at least as long as the revolutionary class consciousness of the industrial proletariat is taken for granted. Political liberties, in their view, bring social grievances into the open (and again the existence of such grievances is taken for granted). Hence the fight for bourgeois democracy is now part of the revolutionary struggle waged by the proletariat, whereas the bourgeoisie, according to Marx, has begun to label all liberal aspirations as socialist.[7] "The general franchise in England," wrote Engels in 1850, "two thirds of whose population consists of industrial proletarians, means the exclusive political rule of the working class with all the revolutionary changes in the social conditions that are inseparably bound up with it."[8]

Another important part of the minimum program worked out by Marx and Engels was their fight against what they considered to be the international bastions of reaction. The chief enemy, and pet hate, of the two friends in this respect was tsarist Russia, and a war against this country or an uprising of its oppressed nationalities was always considered desirable.[9]

Finally, the minimum program entails the systematic debunking and destruction of religion, patriotism, belief in reform, and all the other ideological obstacles which barred the road to true revolutionary class consciousness. In other words, the immediate aims of the movement included an educational mission, for only a truly class-conscious proletariat could be expected to make revolution. As a matter of fact, only class-conscious proletarians were considered good material for a revolutionary party; hence Marx's refusal to include promises for higher wages into the program of the French party. If the French workers needed to be enticed into the movement by unrealistic promises of that kind, he did not want them to join. A complementary part of this educational effort was a constant bitter factional strife against all those who did not share the Marxian view. As it turned out, some of the most ardent intellectual and organizational battles were, in the opinion of Marx, fought against those who wanted to go faster than conditions permitted. For Marx now visualized a comparatively slow process of education and organization, a very gradual inculcation of revolutionary spirit into the working class. He fulminated against his ultra-left opponents in the name of realism: "In place of a critical conception the minority puts the dogmatic, in place of the material conception it puts the idealistic. Instead of the real conditions, mere will becomes for it the driving force of the revolution. Whereas we say to the workers, 'You have to go through fifteen, twenty, fifty years of civil wars and national struggles, not only to change conditions but also to change yourselves and to make yourselves capable of political rule,' you say, on the contrary, 'We must attain to power immediately or we might as well lie down and sleep.' Whereas we point out specifically to the German workers the undeveloped state of the German proletariat, you flatter the national feelings and the German artisans' prejudice of estate in the crudest manner, which is, of course, more popular. Just as the Democrats have turned the word 'people' into a sacred thing, you have done with the word 'proletariat.' Like the Democrats, you substitute the revolutionary phrase for the revolutionary development." [10] Again, what is most important here is the implicit admission that the image of the proletariat on which the Marxist ideas of the 1840's were based has turned out to be a misconception. Yet this is glossed over by the confidence, also implicit, that the proletariat will catch up with itself and, through fifteen or twenty or fifty years of struggle, become "itself."

So much for the minimum program. But all the while the maximum aim of proletarian revolution was never forgotten; on the contrary, while the movement pursued its short-range aims, it should simultaneously take steps toward the maximum program. Even while the Marxist works to liberate bourgeois democracy in its purest and most unadulterated form, he strives also to weaken the bourgeois order itself. He makes ideological attacks on the capitalist way of life and its theories, and he encourages all sorts of rebellion, even the most reactionary type. A conflict of aims between these policies and those of the minimum program proper becomes clearly apparent here. Yet this latent conflict too is glossed over by the optimism with which Marx and Engels continued to believe that the proletarian revolution would occur in the not too distant future. In general, they expected this revolution to start in England. There the peasantry, which they considered the most reactionary of all classes, had been virtually eliminated; real property was concentrated in few hands and could more easily be nationalized than anywhere else. Capitalism had become the prevailing mode of production in most branches of the economy. A large proportion of the population had been converted into wage laborers; trade unions had been formed, and the class struggle between capital and labor had developed to a certain extent. Moreover, Marx and Engels also took it for granted that a proletarian revolution would be more effective in England than anywhere else. For, since England dominated the world market, an English revolution would, they thought, immediately turn into a world revolution. "The English," concluded Marx, "possess all the necessary *material preconditions* of the social revolution. What they lack is the *spirit of generalization* and *revolutionary passion*. Only the General Council is able to inculcate them and thus to speed up a truly revolutionary movement in this country and consequently everywhere . . ." [11] Even this is a change from the expectations held before 1848. Then it had been believed that the proletarian revolution could only be a really international event seizing all the civilized world at once. "Big industry," Engels wrote in 1847, "by the very fact of creating the world market, has established so close a connection between all the nations of the globe, particularly the civilized ones, that every single nation is dependent on what happens to the other. Furthermore, it has equalized social developments in all civilized countries to such an extent that in all these countries the bourgeoisie and the proletariat have become the two decisive classes of society, and the struggle between them, the chief struggle of the moment. The communist revolution will therefore be not merely a national event, but will take place *simultaneously in all civilized countries, i.e., at least in England, America, France, and Germany.* In each of these countries it will develop more rapidly or slowly, depending on whether a given country possess a more highly developed industry, greater wealth, or a more significant amount of productive forces. Hence it will be carried out with slower speed and greater difficulties in Germany, and more rapidly and easily in England. It will also exercize significant influence on the remaining countries of the world; their previous mode of development will be entirely changed and very much accelerated. *It is a universal revolution and will therefore have a world-wide arena."* [12]

The Great Ambivalence

To Marx and Engels this new emphasis on strategy and this distinction between minimal and maximal programs was nothing but the injection of a bit of time lag into the scheme of development elaborated before 1848. From a mere theory of revolution the emphasis was shifted to the strategy of actually working toward revolution. The change in emphasis may have seemed slight. Yet it had momentous implications for the entire structure of Marxian ideas. For, as the European scene was surveyed, as the chances for revolution faded away and the hard labor of working toward revolution was undertaken, the optimistic belief in spontaneous progress was shattered. And with this, one of the basic underpinnings of the Marxist theory of development — the monistic idea of the unity of theory and practice — crumbled. Increasing misery and class consciousness, capital accumulation and crisis, do not develop in step with each other; hence the idea of the unity of theory and practice is transformed from a *belief* or *assumption* into an aspiration, from a statement of alleged fact into a wish. Theory is no longer a mere reflection of actual relationships, a reflection which at most serves as the last link in unifying the proletariat by formulating its latent class consciousness. Theory now anticipates practice and seeks to promote it. Yet, following the demand for a unity of theory and practice, theory must strive constantly not to overshoot the possibilities for effective action; it must remain realisic. With this, idea and reality, aim and movement, freedom and necessity have come in conflict with each other.

As long as Marxism was a theory of revolution, the aims of the movement, the program it proposed to the workers, was clear and unambiguous. Now, with the distinction between maximal and minimal program, ambivalence and ambiguity become the most characteristic features of Marxism, and, really for the first time, dialectics as the language of contradiction comes into its own.

Dialectical images had been used to phrase the original theory of revolution. There was the emphasis on a developmental view and the theory that new institutions, new forms of social organization grew out of the contradictions developing in the old society. With this there came the general awareness of contradictions, that is, irreconcilable strains and stresses in every social system. Finally, dialectical terminology could be applied in the effort to substitute the functional approach for cause-and-effect analysis. Yet the Hegelian jargon was little used, simply because it was not necessary. The analysis of the capitalist system yielded a view of its difficulties and struggles; and the anthropological assumptions underlying the method sufficed to explain why a solution of humanity's problems was possible and even inevitable.

Turning to value judgments, we see that the evaluation of any institution or any historic period was comparatively easy. Everything that had been created in the process of history had, in the beginning, been progressive when compared with what had preceded; and everything had, in due time, become obsolete, a dead form in which life was cramped, and which would, also in due time, be thrown on history's scrap heap. Specifically, capitalism, once a progressive system in comparison to feudalism and slave society, had accomplished all it could, had produced all the benefits which human society could ever derive from it. Most important, it had created all the necessary preconditions for a really human society. But its old, dead forms remained to stifle the further progress of mankind. This is what Marx called the "absolute contradiction between the technical necessities of Modern Industry, and the social character inherent in its capitalistic form." [13] And it is this contradiction which enabled Marx to combine his endorsement of the machine age with his critique of capitalist society. This attitude is poignantly expressed in the following passage:

. . . machinery, considered alone, shortens the hours of labor, but when in the service of capital, lengthens them; . . . in itself it lightens labour, but when employed by capital, heightens the intensity of labour; . . . in itself it is a victory of man over the forces of nature, but in the hands of capital, makes man the slave of those forces; . . . in itself it increases the wealth of the producers, but in the hands of capital makes them paupers. . . .[14]

The removal of these ingrown relationships might be a painful surgical operation during which blood would be lost, but a long-range view would discover the liberating effect it would have. In short, it was very easy to say what was good and what was bad in the present setup. Everything pertaining to the capitalist system of social relations was bad; only modern technology and the working class were good things. There was, indeed, a slight ambivalence concerning the proletariat: it, too, was not an end in itself, but only a tool which would have to disappear, as a class, as soon as its mission had been accomplished. So that the final mission of the proletariat was its self-destruction. But this problem, which, according to Marx, no ruling class could ever solve, would find its solution this time; for the proletariat would actually destroy itself by the very fact of destroying bourgeois society.

Now, however, Marxism gradually develops the starkest ambivalence toward everything that exists.[15] This ambivalence is a direct result of the split mind that develops when a short-range (minimum) and a long-range (maximum) program are formulated and pursued simultaneously. The very distinction made between these two programs means that, according to Marxist theory, there is no straight and unambiguous road toward the attainment of the final goal. Instead a devious route, seemingly leading in an opposite direction, has to be taken. So that the

Marxist, having both directions in mind with equal awareness, is actually moving both forward and backward at the same time; and everything that exists, every social group, institution, ideology, or tradition is at once both conducive to progress and to retrogression. Thus the strengthening of bourgeois democracy, so-called, is progressive because it frees capitalism from its semifeudal political fetters and brings out the struggle between the bourgeoisie and the proletariat; but it is also condemned as soon as the Marxist speaks as a socialist. Bernstein cleverly illustrates the Marxian ambivalence toward the democratic state by recalling that the words "bourgeois" and "citizen" are homonymous in the German language, both being expressed by the word *Bürger*. Hence the concept of the *bürgerliche* state expressed both the dictatorship of the bourgeoisie, which is to be abolished, and the reign of all the citizens' general will, through which he hopes the aims of socialism will be achieved.[16]

And so, the minimum goal is pursued, however vigorously, with latent doubts and misgivings. On the other hand, just because it is pursued vigorously, little thought should be wasted on dreams about long-range ends. It is very well to expose the destruction of human values in capitalist society and thus to pose beautiful humanistic ideals; but the active pursuit of such ideals, the wish to see them realized at once can only defeat the immediate purpose of the movement, the struggle for minimum goals. So that the Marxist who thirsts for action on behalf of these short-range goals tends to shove aside with impatience the ultimate ideals of his doctrine, calling them useless ideological ballast. Instead, he develops a hard-headed pragmatism which expresses itself in the attitude that squeamishness about the methods employed for the sake of reaching the final goal amounts to a betrayal of that goal. Evil means must be used to fight against the features of an evil past. And the best policy is to admit this outright: the class struggle is an era of violence; and its first result is to be a government of violence, the dictatorship of the proletariat.

This tendency to disregard the ultimate ideals inherent in the doctrine is often mitigated, first, by a natural reticence to be as starkly honest as the above statements imply, and, second, by the strong attachments which Marx and the best of his followers have shown to the aesthetic and moral values that form our Western heritage. Their own hard-headedness was often in conflict with their refined taste or their genuine predilection for democratic processes. In consequence, the tendency has been powerful among Marxists to rationalize their lack of squeamishness by pretending, to themselves as well as to others, that the methods they proposed were not at all in conflict with traditional Western values. Here too we notice an almost unbearable ambivalence toward their own means of action.

At the same time, the tendency to disregard their own ideals is strengthened by a strong puritanic streak, which may, perhaps, be traced to Marxist egalitarian principles. The arguments supporting this ascetic predisposition are never made explicit, but can easily be reconstructed. Why — so the Marxists seem to argue — should anyone enjoy the finer things in life, art, music, intellectual stimulation, and so forth, as long as the most blatant inequalities in the distribution of bare necessities have not been redressed? Is it not immoral to enjoy these pleasures while the masses are needy? Thus the pursuit of higher values comes to be seen as one of the subtlest aspects of exploitation. Or else, enjoyment that is not based on material privilege, enjoyment in spite of material poverty, is regarded as an opiate. The proletarian who has a revolution to fight should not waste his time and energy in immaterial or imaginary pleasures.

In the course of the decades around the turn of the century, the Marxist movement began to split into moderate and radical factions, into those who advocated policies of going slowly and those who demanded all-out proletarian offensives. We are probably not wrong if we say that the difference between the two tendencies was essentially their disagreement over the relative weight that should be given to the maximum and minimum programs. As we shall see, both factions showed marked inclinations to let one of these programs swallow up the other one.

Many problems of strategy that were discussed, very heatedly, by the contending factions within the Marxist camp began to revolve around the problem of *maturity*. The question was: Is our society ripe for revolution? Is it ripe for any independent proletarian activity of any political sort? And what are the indications of such a state of ripeness? At what stage should capitalism be pronounced ripe for such revolutionary activity — at its peak, before reaching its peak, or after the beginning of its decline?

To many Marxists, maturity was primarily an attribute of capitalist society. Others spoke of the proletariat as the social force that must attain maturity before it could enter the political scene. The latter could not help seeing a very definite difference between socialists and proletarians, between class-conscious leaders and helplessly alienated working masses — a conception which went diametrically counter to the original Marxist conception of the proletariat. The question became one of how to bridge this gulf between the enlightened leaders from among bourgeois intellectuals and the unenlightened proletariat, caught in petty-bourgeois sentiments. Should the leaders patiently and confidently await the inevitable growth of the proletariat to political maturity? Should they try to promote class consciousness? Or should they despair entirely of the workers' ability to attain it and therefore endeavor to manipulate them into revolutionary action? These burning questions, which came to shake the Marxist movement to its foundation and divide it hopelessly and irreconcilably, were intimately linked with the problem of party organization, an issue over which socialists and communists first developed their differences. Thus the importance of the party organization was questioned by radicals of the type of Rosa Luxemburg who took Marx at his word and banked their hopes on the spontaneous actions of the class-conscious proletarian masses. The defenders of strict proletarian discipline, on the other hand, tended to frown on spontaneous mass action of any sort and considered the party apparatus as the only way in which rational decision-making could be assured for the proletarian revolution.[17]

The ambivalent appraisal of political democracy was intimately linked with this issue. For the question was, whether the "maturity of material conditions" by definition included broad constitutional democracy. Did any independent activity on the part of the working class make sense under preconstitutional conditions?

If it did not, then the minimum program of working for democratic reforms had to be adopted. But if it did make sense, then,
perhaps, the very idea of a minimum program was false. Some
Marxists came to think that the fight for democracy was at best
a marginal issue, or, at worst, served to deflect the proletariat
from its more real ultimate goals.

If the place of constitutional democracy in the action program
of the working-class movement was thus questioned, the same
doubts applied to reforms and improvements of any kind. Reforms might improve the workingmen's lot; they might even
improve his ability to make revolution, by clearing the way and
removing obstacles. But reforms were also a diversion from the
real aim. They might lull the proletariat into acquiescence, might
soften it, and render it permanently useless for revolutionary
struggle.

In short, the question was over the importance of the minimum
program. Though few Marxists questioned the need to distinguish
between minimal and maximal aims, never-ending controversies
broke out which were essentially over the weight to be given to
the minimum program. All the leaders of the Marxist movement
may have been in agreement that the movement must carry on
its fight. All of them may even have been in agreement that
certain specific methods should characterize the fight of the
working class; for instance, few leaders questioned the utility of
the strike as a specifically proletarian weapon. But the agreement
ended right there. For there was disagreement over all questions
connected with strikes. Should they be undertaken only for very
specific aims, and if so, were these aims political or economic?
Or should they be regarded as a means by which to further
revolutionary developments in general, in which case the strike
would only be a preparatory step in the revolutionary process?
In that event it would matter little whether any particular strike
turned out to be a success or a failure. While many leaders of
the Marxist movement insisted that strikes should be undertaken
only if they had a fair chance of bringing benefits to the workers,
others held, on the contrary, that what looked like a failure in the
short run might well turn out to be a success in the long run.
An unsuccessful strike might set the proletariat back in their

living standard, might empty the coffers of their union, or lead to political oppression. But these setbacks might serve as an object lesson in the nature of capitalism and therefore be a psychological advance, while the experience of concerted mass action would take the movement further on the road toward maturity.[18]

If even a general strike was no more than a means by which to deepen a revolutionary crisis, what form would the actual revolution take? How, specifically, would the working class seize power? More clearly than anything else, the different answers that were given to this question showed some of the depth of the gulf which separated the different factions in their attempt to weigh the importance of the minimum and maximum programs against each other. Theoretically, it was easy, perhaps, to make a neat distinction between the two programs and between different methods of political struggle. The fight for constitutional reforms, and the struggle for economic concessions, waged within the framework of constitutional democracy, could be seen quite apart from the final seizure of power, when the workers would man the barricades and establish their proletarian dictatorship. But what if the fight for democracy had to be waged by similarly manning the barricades? Or what if the seizure of power would take the perfectly legal and peaceful means of an electoral victory? In both cases the distinction between the two programs would largely disappear. The minimum and maximum programs would merge into each other; or else one would be swallowed by the other and disappear.

The paradox was particularly great for those who held that even the proletarian revolution would take the constitutional forms of a victory at the polls. What was not seen by many Marxists who took this attitude was that this did away with the very concept of revolution. All those who insisted on this democratic form of a proletarian revolution, arguing that the growth of democracy was the surest and only indication of political and social maturity, were really saying that the revolution was no longer necessary as soon as it became possible and advisable, and that it was not advisable as long as it was still necessary. This paradox found one of its classical expressions in what Engels had to say about the general strike:

At the Geneva Alliancist Congress of September 1, 1873, the problem of the general strike played a great role; only everyone admitted that the complete organization of the working class and a full kitty were necessary prerequisites for it. And here is just the catch. On the one hand, the governments, particularly if we encourage them by political reticence, will never let the organizations or the cash funds of the workers develop that far; on the other hand, political events and the offensive measures of the ruling classes will lead to the liberation of the workers long before the proletariat succeeds in acquiring this ideal organization and this colossal reserve fund. If they had them, however, they would not need the general strike in order to attain their goal.[19]

The entire complex of problems centering around the question of maturity, and all the ambivalences resulting from the existence of two parallel programs, were results of the destruction of the monistic belief in the unity of theory and practice. Similar ambivalences, ambiguities, and contradictions arose in every part of the Marxist structure of ideas. In the following chapter we shall illustrate some of the most significant of these conflicts by a brief survey of the development of the Marxist movement in Western Europe. For the history of Marxism after 1848, and particularly after 1890, is the history of the disintegration of the basic unity of the Marxist system of ideas.

Chapter Six

The Marxist House Divided

Words are wise men's counters, they do but reckon by them; but they are the money of fools, that value them by the authority of an Aristotle, a Cicero, or a Thomas, or any other doctor what-soever, if but a man.   Thomas Hobbes

The Changing Nature of the Working-Class Movement

The history of Marxist socialism in Europe up to the First World War might be divided, roughly, into three periods. The first begins with the failure of the 1848 revolution and ends with the abortive Paris Commune of 1871. The second extends, approximately, to the late 'eighties or early 'nineties; its end, and the beginning of the third period, is marked by such events as the death of Marx, the founding of the Second International, and the repeal of Bismarck's antisocialist laws in Germany.

During the first period the feeling that the revolution is imminent persists very strongly, and every new domestic crisis, every new war brings hopes to Marx and Engels that the proletarian revolution, which 1848 did not produce, would soon burst out. Yet the optimism of the 'forties has been tempered. It is now balanced by the realization that the class struggle might turn out to be long and arduous before the old order is finally smashed. In addition, the view now prevails that the proletariat is still little prepared for its historic mission; hence the importance of the Party and the First International as a nucleus of really class-conscious (that is, history-conscious) leaders, organizers, and teachers. Having thought of themselves as spokesmen for a really existing mass movement, the small group of intellectuals that follow Marx now vigorously strive to find themselves a mass basis. For that purpose they ally themselves with other radical groups, though only as long as they can ultimately dominate them; hence the violent personal and factional squabbles that were to help break up the First International. Turning to look at the working man himself, we find that only now labor movements begin to organize themselves. Moreover, the movements that do get started are not in touch with, or influenced by, Marxist doctrines. The English trade unions hardly knew of Marx's existence. The German workers were organized by Lasalle and, in France, the proletariat seemed to follow Proudhon and Blanqui.

The period between the two Internationals marks the low ebb of proletarian socialism in Europe as capitalism flourishes in an unprecedentedly spectacular boom, and the Western world sets out on a feverish race of colonial expansion. In Germany, Bismarck uses the carrot and the big stick (social security legislation and repressive antisocialist laws) to tame the working class movement. And while thus the practice of the movement is utterly stultified, theory turns away from problems of the revolution and goes its own ways. Marx sets out to write volumes II, III, and IV of his economic analysis of the capitalist system, a task which is never finished, while Engels deals with problems of military strategy and international relations, and attempts to elaborate the philosophy of dialectical materialism. Surely, the unity of theory and practice here is not even a dream!

The third period, however, seems to bring with it a reversal of the trend and a real unification of the labor movement with Marxist ideology, at least on the continent. In England Marxism completely failed to strike roots, but in France, Germany, and Russia, the workers begin to rally under its banner. In 1880 Marx has the satisfaction of dictating the program of the first proletarian party, identifying itself with him. Like the Erfurt program of the German party written in 1891 and the program of the Russian party which followed soon afterwards, the platform of the French party is the minimum program of the movement; but the long-range aims are set forth in the preambles. In France, in consequence of this definition of minimal aims the anarchists, impatient with gradualism, split definitely from the social-democratic movement.

From the glosses Engels wrote on the Erfurt platform, we know that he criticized it on several counts. Nonetheless, he seems, on the whole, to have been extremely confident that Marxist ideology, in all its pureness, would in the end be adopted entirely by the labor movement on the continent, and especially in Germany. If he underestimated the difficulties of this marriage of the theory and practice, it may have been because he underestimated the changes that had taken place in Europe in the forty-odd years since the publication of the Communist Manifesto, changes that had deeply affected the continental working class and that should similarly have affected Marxist doctrine.

In brief, the German working movement which appeared to rally wholeheartedly under the Marxian program was essentially a trade union movement in composition and organization, as well as leadership; and, for better or for worse, this trade union character could not but affect the real aims for which it struggled. Its fight was mainly one for social justice to be achieved within the framework of the existing society. And it is easy to see why the German trade unions were steadily losing the revolutionary spirit. In spite of the grievances which the proletariat still had, in spite of the viciousness with which the worker may have been treated in various respects, and in spite of the insecurities of the business cycle, it could not be denied that the social and economic position of the industrial laborer had infinitely improved in the second half of the nineteenth century. Bismarck's social security legislation had softened the hardships of capitalism for the individual workers' families; the avalanche growth of the industrial working population had multiplied the ranks of the labor movement and given it a sense of political confidence, while the coffers of the unions had swelled. The trade union movement had begun to branch out into the most varied activities affecting all aspects of the workers' lives, and had developed complex organizational structures. The European economy as a whole, finally, was undergoing a tremendous boom, and the working class could not but benefit from the unprecedented wealth that was being amassed by the nation. All this gave the worker a decided vested interest in the existing system and predisposed him to gradualism. It is significant that since the abolition of Bismarck's antisocial laws, the German party, along with all other parties in the Second International, except the Russian, renounced all illegal activity on general principle.

Yet, this comparatively tame trade union movement insistently identified itself with revolutionary Marxism. In retrospect, we can therefore discover amazing discrepancies between its ideology and its actual behavior. Vigorous confessions of solidarity with the international proletariat were in fact hiding a growing anxiousness on the part of the movement to demonstrate its loyalty to dynasty and Reich; the sharpening international rivalries which finally led to the world wars of our century were already beginning to hollow out supranational class solidarities. Similarly, the movement stubbornly stuck to theories of the inevitability of revolution even while it acquired greater and greater vested interests in democracy, so that, instead of fighting for the proletarian dictatorship, it was fighting more and more for an extension of the franchise. Marx had said that the proletariat had been cast outside capitalist society and that it would not liberate itself without smashing all the social relationships and institutions of the old social structure. The German Social-Democratic Party and its trade-union apparatus, on the other hand, was turning into a state within the state, which sought to shape all aspects of its citizens' lives. The German worker was developing political, economic, and cultural institutions for himself, which existed side by side with parallel bourgeois institutions. There were social-democratic coöperatives in the field of retail trade and insurance; there was a vast press empire and a network of sports clubs, youth organizations, educational institutions. All this meant no more than that the workers' movement had turned into the most carefully and elaborately organized *pressure group within the existing social framework*; a bureaucratic hierarchy which came to acquire a life and meaning of its own. Instead of being no more than the brain-center of the proletarian revolution, it became the embodiment of numerous vested interests for administrators, journalists, trade-union officials, and an army of white collar employees. With this, it was only natural that the organization, as such, gradually developed the greatest resistance against revolutionary aspirations and plans. As the era of violent repression gave way to an age of economic concessions and political victories, the personnel, the tactics, and the whole tradition of the workers' movement underwent a change. The conspiratorial traditions of the 'seventies were quickly forgotten. The movement acquired a good deal of "respectability."

All these observations can be made with comparative clarity fifty years later. In the 'nineties, however, the socialists and their bourgeois antagonists alike were deceived by the insistence with which the movement upheld the letter of Marxian revolutionary doctrines. Shortly before the turn of the century, however, one group of leaders made a surprising attempt to revise the theories of the movement so as to make them conform to the changed conditions and practices. Called *revisionism*, this rebel school of socialist theory decided to call things by their right names even at the risk of being called traitors to Marxism.

The Revisionist Rebellion

One of the principal assertions the revisionists made was that socialism could be attained without a revolution by purely economic pressure. This, they claimed, applied even in the German Reich with its monarchic constitution; even there no violent shifts in power, no democratic revolution was required. Collective bargaining, plus tactical collaboration with bourgeois liberalism, would suffice. The concept of socialism was redefined to mean the fight for social reforms, which meant the abandonment of all ideas of revolution and proletarian dictatorship. The working class was to be one of the pressure groups in a democratic constitutional system, and not a class virtually outside society. With the notion of relentless class warfare the old ideas of international class solidarity also went overboard. The socialists, too, had a fatherland, according to the revisionist school; and their struggle for reform was conceived as a purely domestic problem. Similarly, it was now acknowledged that national loyalty should override class loyalty, so that a national emergency must lead to the abandonment of domestic struggles. In short, the old notions of class warfare were being supplanted by a theory of class co-operation and conciliation.

Attitudes like these were accompanied, and to a certain degree rationalized, by a thorough critique of the Marxian analysis of capitalist society and the Marxian theory of revolution. A major argument of the revisionists was the assertion that Marxian theories of breakdown and increasing misery had been disproven by actual developments. "Definite signs of an economic world crash of unprecedented violence cannot be found, nor can one say that the intermediate periods of prosperity are becoming much shorter," wrote Bernstein.[1] And when Karl Kautsky pleaded that such an analysis would mean the end of the Marxian socialist dreams, Bernstein replied that, on the contrary, the spread and distribution and the gradual equalization of property which his analysis implied would bring practical socialism nearer. On the other hand, if by "socialist dreams" Kautsky meant the vision of a classless and stateless society brought about by a proletarian revolution, he was entirely right; this vision should be abandoned.[2] Thus Bernstein, in practice, redefined socialism to mean the Marxian minimum program, and was prepared to discard the maximal aims as utopian. "The final aim," he wrote, "whatever it may be, is nothing to me; the movement, everything." In line with this, we notice a tendency to make the terms socialism and democracy more and more synonymous, so that the fight for the latter can be regarded, *ipso facto*, as a fight for the former. As Bernstein wrote, "The idea of democracy includes, in the conception of the present day, a notion of justice — an equality of rights for all members of the community." [3] Note the phrase "the idea of democracy"; did Bernstein wish to imply that, in actual practice, democracy had not carried with it that social justice for which the movement is fighting? Did he mean that, in actual practice, democracy was not enough? By no means! In the preface to the 1899 edition of his famous book he points out that the degree of democratization actually achieved is an excellent barometer of the proletariat's political maturity. The attainment of political influence in the democratic process is the surest sign that the proletariat is mature enough to assume political responsibilities. "Democracy is at any given time as much government by the working classes as these are capable of practicing according to their intellectual maturity and the degree of social democracy they have attained." [4] The implication is clear: if the actual achievements of the socialist movement have so far been inadequate, the fault lies not with the system but with the proletariat. The system makes sure that every class attains as much influence as it deserves. This is indeed a far cry from the Marxian critique of bourgeois society!

But the revisionist critique of Marxism does not stop here. Bernstein attacked the entire economic interpretation of history, which he interpreted narrowly as a cause-and-effect theory of economic determinism. Fighting against this conception — or misconception, he claimed that economic facts do not determine everything; economic development was merely one factor, although perhaps one of the most important, determining historical processes. Other factors may be of very great importance too, and they should not be neglected. "One must give full consideration not only to the development and influence of the forces of production and relations of production, but also the conceptions of law and morals, the historical and religious traditions of an era, the influence of geographical and other natural influences in which must be included the nature of man himself and his mental capacities." [5]

Finally, Bernstein attacked dialectics as animistic hocus-pocus. He criticized the notion of inevitability through a concerted attack on the theories of breakdown, crisis, and increasing misery. And he swept down with fury on the idea alleged to be the essence of dialectics, that matter have purpose inherent in it. This teleology was seen as a myth and as self-deception. Reality, he maintained, is not inevitably marching toward the ideal. Yet Bernstein still considered it morally desirable that the existing system be removed or improved; and revisionists, in general, pride themselves on being moralists instead of fatalists. As Max Eastman writes: "It is easy to scorn your own ideals, treating them as mere signs of a crisis in the evolution of material forces, when you have already confided the attainment of your ideals to those material forces. That was the hardheadedness of Marx and Engels. . . . To be hardheaded in this real world, which cares nothing at all about what you consider higher, and yet at the same time be idealistic and fight to make something higher out of it, is a little more difficult." [6] Here we see at last a strict separation between value and science, between ideals and reality, which completely contradicts what Marx and Engels had asserted and demanded. We see the restoration of a dualism of purpose and implementation. According to Eastman, the most brilliant American exponent of revisionist ideas, the social engineer first sets himself a purpose and then applies science to see how that purpose might best be achieved. According to Marxist doctrines, purpose was derived scientifically; a scientific appraisal of real conditions led to the formulation of purpose, and both science and purpose supposedly reflected the real movement of social forces in capitalist society. Now, after it has become apparent that this "real movement" was misjudged from the very beginning, science and purpose go their different and mutually contradictory way; they have little to do with each other any longer. As a consequence, Marxism is divided into a set of purposes which are unscientific (the socialist ideal) on the one hand, and a scientific method (economic determinism), which is quite independent of purpose and ideals, on the other. Either one or the other has, by various people, been named as the essence of Marxism. Henri de Man, for instance, claims that socialism is not scientific at all, but is moral; that its origin is not in the class structure but in a completely subjective feeling of guilt or shame. In short, the revisionists do not believe in the Marxian prognosis and therefore claim that they are fighting for socialism purely from moral conviction. The orthodox school that arose against them, conversely, was convinced of the inevitability of socialism. Just for that reason, however, they could cast out all ideas of morality, and many of them in actual fact proposed that the proletariat could sit still waiting while the inevitable course of history would work itself out. Both revisionism and orthodoxy, however, were united in making a strict separation of socialism from historical materialism. "The theory of Marxism as well as its practice are free from judgments of value. It is therefore false to conceive as it is widely done, intra et extra muros, that Marxism and Socialism are as such identical. For logically, regarded as a scientific system and apart from its historical effect, Marxism is only a theory of the laws of the movement of society formulated in general terms. . . . . But insight into the validity of Marxism, which included insight into the necessity of Socialism, is by no means a matter of value judgements and just as little an indication of practical procedure. For it is one thing to recognize a necessity, and another thing to work for this necessity. It is quite possible for someone convinced of the final victory of Socialism to fight against it." [7] Similarly, we have seen that it was possible for someone convinced in the staying power of capitalism, as Bernstein was, to fight against it.

Orthodox Marxism

Revisionism thus attempted to adjust socialist theory to the actual practices of the labor movement and boldly challenged Marxism as a scientific theory. A vigorous response was given at once by those whom we shall call the *orthodox* Marxists. This label should be applied with great care, because the group it is meant to symbolize was extremely amorphous, certainly not a distinct school within the Marxist camp. There is no authoritative representative of orthodox Marxism, even though Karl Kautsky, who is here cited almost to the exclusion of all others, is certainly one of the most prominent of those that are covered by the label.[8] Nor is there an unwavering or unambiguous orthodox interpretation. Instead, there was a marked tendency on the part of those here called orthodox to make a decided stand against revisionism at first but, gradually, to make important adjustments under the fire of revisionist criticism. Thus the first response to Bernstein's heretical prognoses was a sharp insistence on the inevitability of a proletarian revolution, a position which was, however, considerably reinterpreted, watered down, or even denied by the same orthodox leaders in later years. Similar developments occurred with regard to other aspects of the doctrine, for instance, in philosophic questions.

The characteristic trait of the orthodox, after all, was not a question of how the doctrine should be interpreted; the mark of orthodoxy was an emotional loyalty to the doctrine, in one form or another. The orthodox were characterized by their attitude that Marxism, despite Bernstein, was the last word in social science and philosophy. As we shall see, this attitude itself leads to contradictory conclusions. On the one hand, it encourages that stubborn insistence on upholding the writings of Marx and Engels to the last letter; on the other hand, it leads to the claim that Marxism can be reconciled with other schools of contemporary science. It is, perhaps, another typical trait of the orthodox that they frequently maintained both these attitudes and remained quite blind to the possibility that they might be in conflict.

The final argument with which the orthodox tended to combat revisionism is extremely revealing. To challenge Marxism, to cast doubt on its scientific correctness, meant to betray the workers' movement. The workers needed their ideology in order to wage their class struggle effectively, and the destruction of the myth in the name of which they were fighting would have served the interest of the bourgeoisie. Marxism thus became a matter of orthodoxy, of proletarian morale and proletarian honor, whereas it had previously been a matter of conviction and scientific investigation. Moreover, the orthodox clearly tended to value Marxist theory for yet another reason: if it was a morale booster for the proletariat, it was also a propaganda weapon against the ruling classes. Marx and Engels, convinced that arguments could achieve little in the struggle between classes, had not thought their ideas would interest any representative of the bourgeoisie; they spoke exclusively to the proletariat. In contrast, the orthodox Marxist around the turn of the century regarded their theories of the inevitability of proletarian revolution as a psychological warfare device by which the ruling classes could be blackmailed into making concessions. Thus the threat of revolution became more important to them than the actual staging of a revolution. In retrospect, this switch from actual warfare to psychological warfare must be regarded as an unmistakable sign of political weakness. Only this change in the nature of the ideology can really explain why the orthodox refused to look the challenge of revisionism square in the eye.[9] We have already mentioned a telling instance of this refusal: Bernstein had pointed out to Kautsky some factual evidence to prove that the Marxian theory of increasing misery was wrong. Kautsky, in turn, did not attempt to disprove Bernstein's facts by adducing better facts of his own; instead, he refused to accept Bernstein's statement on the ground that it ran counter to his, Kautsky's, cherished dreams of inevitable socialism: "If that were true," he argues, "we should never reach our goal. If the number of capitalists were to grow, not that of the dispossessed, we should get further and further away from our goal the more that development would go on: Capitalism, not Socialism, would then be strengthened." [10]

In their effort to combat the heresies of revisionism, the orthodox at first sharply rejected any notion of returning to Kant[11] and his dualistic philosophy. Hence there could be no admission that Marxism consisted of a moral philosophy and a social theory that were independent of each other; nor could it be admitted that it was primarily a moral philosophy, linked to a basically unscientific theory. The only other possible stand to take was to declare it to be a completely amoral social science. If the revisionists had regarded Marxism as a myth, the orthodox regarded it as the last word in social science.[12] The orthodox Marxist has developed that self-satisfied assurance which is behind the well-known *Marxistenlächeln* — the supercilious smirk of one who knows all the answers. And if he wants to call any statement unscientific, he labels it un-Marxian. Once this claim is made, there is no more room for any biases, any emotional attitudes or moral judgments that might be injected into the doctrine. But with this comes the task of reconciling the doctrine with other contemporary contributions to social science; and indeed, for the last fifty-odd years many orthodox Marxists have made an effort to show that Marxism in no essential way contradicted the contributions of positivism, pragmatism, liberalism, psychology, and other contemporary doctrines; there is a whole flock of writers who have tried to make Marxism palatable to the modern scientist.

Two devices were used by the orthodox school to reconcile Marxism with other contemporary theories. Certain disturbing features had to be explained away; and certain features that had so far been lacking in the doctrine had to be incorporated. It is the orthodox school which set out to extend Marxism into the most varied disciplines of social science. Just as the German Social-Democratic Party developed its own institutions and services to cover all the daily pursuits of the worker, so the party's ideology branches out, and a Marxist anthropology, a Marxist aesthetics, and, last but not least, a Marxist school of natural science develop. The thoroughness with which Marxism is made to branch out into disciplines and areas for which it was not intended is no Soviet invention, but a development that started in the German Social-Democratic Movement, and, in reality, with Engels, who might well be called the first orthodox Marxist.

Among features that might be explained away one of the most disturbing was dialectics. Karl Kautsky, perhaps the outstanding theorist of the German orthodox school, had two conceptions of dialectics. One of these conceptions is of dialectics as the metabolism of the individual with his environment,[13] where the synthesis is the mutual adjustment of the clash between the ego and the environment. Little attention is paid either to the dialectics of the class struggle or to any distinction between natural and social, or man-made, environments. Hence this is a nature-dialectics much more than a dialectics of history; and it does not astonish us to hear, after this, that Kautsky began his intellectual development as a Darwinist natural scientist. Another interpretation of dialectics adopted by Kautsky expounds it as a creative thought process. Engels had regarded contradictions as something objective; they were contradictions in the material environment, and the source of development, therefore, was a struggle between contradictory objects. According to Kautsky, however, contradictions and incompatibilities are a consequence of inadequacies in man's intellect; they are nothing but inadequacies in definition. Dialectics, then, is the creative thought process which seeks definitions that will make seemingly incompatible phenomena appear compatible. Synthesis is thus the adjustment of thoughts to one another. That neither of these interpretations has very much to do with the Marxian concept of dialectics should be obvious to the reader.

Another disturbing feature that begged to be explained away, if Marxism was to be reconciled with modern social science, was the concept of inevitability. Revisionism had attacked Marxism for developing this concept. The orthodox school turns against this attack by claiming that Marx never was so foolish as to claim socialism to be inevitable. Marx never said that the accumulation of misery, chronic crisis, the breakdown of capitalism, and the social revolution would come as certainly as Judgment Day; all these developments are only trends, and the coming of socialism is only something very much to be desired or something that is possible. Here, as in many other instances, we note that, in effect, the orthodox school comes close to agreeing with the revisionists; the difference is only that the latter refuse to derive their views from Marx, whereas the former refuse to abandon him. Both groups reject the theory of breakdown in favor of a theory of peaceful, democratic, smooth evolution from capitalism to socialism; but revisionism did this in opposition to Marx, whereas the orthodox reinterpret Marxism to fit their evolutionary theories and their reformist policies.

In short, the orthodox school claimed that their method was the same as that of Marx, only it yielded new conclusions today, and called for different policies. If Marx had called on the proletariat to smash the bourgeois state, the current aim of the movement was to take it over. Explaining the change, Kautsky maintained that before the bourgeois-democratic revolution, politics had been a struggle between different exploiting classes; the exploited could join the political arena only by overthrowing the state of the ruling classes and creating themselves a state of their own. But today, he continued, the state has, first of all, acquired functions that are vital to the well-being of the exploited; hence the working masses have a vested interest in preserving it. Moreover, the class struggle can now take place within the existing political framework of constitutional democracy. The seizure of power now means nothing else than winning a majority within the existing state, so that future revolutions will be revolutions by consent. No other revolution is recognized by Kautsky any longer: "Where the conditions that make the general franchise into a means for the liberation of the proletariat are lacking, *all* conditions for this liberation are lacking. Marx was not one of those who seek a means toward liberation effective under all circumstances, whether the social conditions were ripe for it or not." [14]

Another device by which Marx was reinterpreted was to use the same terms but give them a new meaning. Thus we have seen that Kautsky still spoke about the proletarian revolution but demanded that it be a tame and civilized revolution. In contrast to Luxemburg's call for a strategy of annihilating the bourgeoisie, (*Vernichtungsstrategie*), he conceived of the party's tasks as one of weakening the bourgeois class by constant harassing (*Ermattungsstrategie*). Whereas the radical wing interpreted the concept of maturity to mean economic and political crisis, to the moderates it meant capitalism at the very peak of its expansion and prosperity. To the left wing, the maturity of the proletariat meant that the working class had developed revolutionary radicalism and organizational discipline; the social-democrats thought of it as the lick and polish of civilized living, a thorough training in democratic constitutionalism, and a certain respectability, which Lenin, Luxemburg, and others of their outlook considered essentially bourgeois. Class consciousness, finally, for the left wingers, meant the will to make revolution, while in the usage of the moderates it took on the meaning of a craftsman's pride, a feeling that the working class had won itself a respected place within the entire society.

Here, then, is the ideology of orthodox Marxism as we have used the term. In contrast to the revisionists, it still maintained the fall of the capitalist system to be virtually inevitable. But like revisionism it developed an aversion to violence and an overriding attachment to the gradualism of the democratic process; hence it, too, spent all its efforts on the struggle for the extension of democracy and the enactment of social legislation. Marxian terminology with its tough language of rebellion was nonetheless preserved, not only because it provided the working class with an allegedly scientific rallying cry; but also, and perhaps more important, Marxist ideology in the hands of the German labor movement became a means by which further concessions could be extorted from the ruling classes. In the name of Marx's scientific analysis, the bourgeoisie could be threatened with inevitable revolution, unless they satisfied the demands of the workers. For this purpose the insistence on the inevitable collapse of capitalism was as essential to the orthodox school as it was a burden to the revisionists. But while the abandonment of the Marxian prognosis prompted many revisionists to vigorous action on behalf of their ideals, the myth of inevitability, the belief in complete determinism tended to lead the orthodox into quietism and inaction. If the peaceful evolution of socialism was predetermined, why spoil things by rash action? At the same time it must be realized that the orthodox at their best had attained a far greater degree of sophisitication than, say, the Engels of the *Anti-Dühring*. The orthodox Marxism of the turn of the century is mellower, less exuberantly optimistic, somewhat more stoical than the two men who founded the movement fifty years before.

The Revival of Radicalism

The orthodox school came into being as a distinguishable strand within the Marxist movement in the years between 1890 and 1910, an era of general prosperity and capitalist expansion, during which the rise of revisionism was only too natural. In those years, its main attacks were directed against the revisionist theories that the democratic revolution was no longer necessary, that the workers' movement ought to ally itself with liberalism, and that the writings of Marx should be freely criticized. But after 1905 the main target of the orthodox became a rebel force on the left wing of the labor movement, characterized by the names of Rosa Luxemburg and Anton Pannekoek. Here arose a group that was dissatisfied with mere reforms, that rebelled against the bureaucratic organization of the Social-Democratic Party, against the alleged stranglehold on the movement of trade-union leaders who had turned into bourgeois politicians, and against the mealy-mouthed lip service paid to the proletarian revolution. Here was a group of leaders who wanted to educate the proletariat for revolution through violent political action. In this last respect it was quite close to syndicalism; but, unlike Sorel, Rosa Luxemburg did not believe theory to be only a myth. She stuck firmly to Marxism as a scientific method, and her entire political life was one momentous attempt to reunite the theory and practice of Marxian socialism in the radical spirit of its founders. Rosa Luxemburg not only tried to rescue the Marxian belief in the breakdown of capitalism, after Karl Kautsky had reëstablished his faith in democracy; she also expected this crisis to break out in the foreseeable future. Moreover, this would be an international crisis rocking the entire civilized world. By personal background as well as in her theoretical writings she had a broad international horizon that went counter to the currents in the Second International. Together with the reëstablishment of the theory of crisis she resurrected a theory of spontaneity which held that the workers themselves would make the proletarian revolution. According to Luxemburg, the intellectuals who lead them have no other function than to act as catalysts of class consciousness. If they took over the movement, if they overorganized it, they would only frustrate something that would develop better without their interference. On this point, as well as on some others, she clashed bitterly with Lenin, who was a great admirer of organization, even though he intended to use it differently from the German Social-democrats.

The practical policies of Luxemburg were marked by a relentless radicalism which brooked no compromises and no opportunism. To her, the proletariat was not to build its own state within the state but was, once again, conceived to be a society outside of the existing capitalist society, which could achieve its own ends only by acting always toward the maximum goal. Yet she did not propose that developments be forced in a fit of impatience. But neither should the proletariat ally itself with forces to which it was ultimately hostile, like the liberals, the peasantry, or national movements. In that sense, Rosa Luxemburg was opposed to the whole idea of a minimum program for the workers' movement, and to the Kautskyan preoccupation with the bourgeois-democratic revolution.[15] Instead, she proposed that the only activity which would educate the proletariat and drive developments further would be continued revolutionary activity, including the favorite weapon of syndicalism, the general strike. If such outbreaks of mass revolt were successful, capitalism would indeed crumble; but even if they failed, they would be a revolutionary school for the workers. In this she took a similar stand to

Marx when he wrote in praise of the abortive Paris Commune. Lenin, the leader of the Bolshevik faction in the Russian Social-Democratic Labor Party, shared Luxemburg's radicalism, and many of his followers were of a mental frame very much like hers. Leninism differs from the ideology of Luxemburg, however, in that it does not share her sanguine optimism. Lenin did not believe, as Luxemburg did, that imperialism would lead to the breakdown of capitalism with inevitable certainty, and he criticized her on this account, arguing that her optimistic conviction led to quietistic conclusions. Nor did he share her belief in the maturity and class-consciousness of the proletariat, her faith in spontaneous revolutionary development which needed the ideological leadership of Marxist scholars only as a psychological catalyst. Instead, Lenin from the very beginning of his revolutionary activities, asserted a fundamental distrust of the working class, and an unwillingness to rely on spontaneous historical forces. Hence his preoccupation with the education of an enlightened general staff to lead the workers into revolution. Hence his stress on problems of organization and his demand that the masses be manipulated into revolutionary action.

In retrospect, one might say that Lenin's pessimism was somewhat more realistic than Luxemburg's bland hopes. But they must, in addition, be explained within the context of the specifically Russian conditions with which Lenin was familiar. When Russian intellectuals made their attempt to apply Marxist doctrines in their backward country, inhabited predominantly by peasants, and ruled by a semi-absolute dynasty, the basic unity of the Marxist ideology broke down even further. Controversies over the minimum program concerned not only the problem of party organization and leadership, but also the question of how best to fight for the bourgeois revolution, still required in tsarist Russia, and the road from such a bourgeois revolution to the next step, the establishment of a proletarian dictatorship.

We have already observed that the trend toward the disintegration of the basic unity of Marxism was reversed after theories of imperialism like those developed by Luxemburg, Hilferding, Lenin, Bukharin, and others, gave Marxism a completely novel orientation. For the first time since Marx, new disruptive and revolutionary tendencies were discovered in the existing order, and the pertinent theoretical reformulations were made at a time when actual movements of revolt were undeniably in preparation. And so, as Marxism in its Leninist version turns its attention to the rising backward nations, a new unity of theory and practice, of social science and radical criticism, is found which gives surprising strength to both Leninist ideology and to colonial movements of revolt.

Nonetheless, the difference between the basic unity achieved by Lenin and that of Marx is significant. Both theories purport to be reflections and articulations of actual mass movements of revolt. But the Marxian proletarian revolution was not only to abolish a specific system of exploitation; it was expected to liberate society at once from all oppressive relationships and usher in a period of truly human history. Nothing like that can even be the dream of anti-imperialist revolutions. There is no highly developed industrial establishment which exploited masses in backward areas might seize in order to run it for the benefit of all mankind. The task of the victorious communist revolution will, instead, be to build up a modern industry as the first precondition of a communist society. This industrialization effort, however, requires for the time being a social system which is as oppressive and exploitative as capitalism itself at its worst. The dictatorship of the proletariat in Russia, as in countries further to the east, bears some resemblance to the England of the industrial revolution, except that the human cost of industrialization in England was to a degree mitigated by checks and balances, parliamentary blue books, and criticism from other classes, whereas the Soviet world has added total control, total ruthlessness, and an entire Orwellian world of thought control and terror. And, paradoxically, Marxism thus turns into a theory of state. The precise stages of this doctrinal evolution will be the topic of another book.

On Two Sides of the Barricades

The outbreak of the war in 1914 made the fundamental break between the Marxist writ and social-democratic practice obvious to all. While individuals like Luxemburg and Liebknecht endeavored to remain faithful to the spirit of class war and international class solidarity, the movement as a whole rallied to support the national war effort not only in Germany but in all other countries except Russia, while orthodox theorists like Kautsky tried against all odds to restore the unity of the movement. By 1917 an Independent Social-Democratic Party broke away from the majority in order to fight for a "peace of understanding." And here the line between revisionism and orthodoxy is obscured beyond recognition, as both schools have their representatives in both of the socialist factions. The revolution of November 1918, moreover, settled one of the most important practical issues between the two groups, namely, whether a democratic proletarian revolution was possible within the framework of the Wilhelminian empire. With the passing of that empire, this issue had become academic, and the conflict that remained was a purely semantic fight between theoretical die-hards on both sides over the issue of whether the Social-Democratic Party of Germany was, in essence, Kantian or Marxian. This was neither very bitter nor very important. Hence in programmatic or ideological statements it could easily be solved by judicious phrasing which glossed over the disagreement to the satisfaction of both sides.[16] And, since there were no longer any serious principal differences over practical policies,· this need not astonish us. Both factions were united in their fight against extremism on both the left and the right, for the sake of defending the democratic republic, disagreeing only over tactical questions.

In practice, this must be regarded as a victory for revisionism. Whenever socialist aims now came into conflict with democratic ideals, Kautsky inevitably opted for democracy, as his grandson correctly emphasizes.[17] In effect, he gave up the very idea of revolution after 1918. Nothing illustrates this so well as a passage he wrote in 1922:

In his famous article on the Critique of the Social-Democratic Party program, Marx says,
"Between the capitalist and the communist society comes a period of revolutionary transition from one to the other. A political transition period corresponds to it, the state of which can be nothing else than the revolutionary dictatorship of the proletariat."

Today, on the basis of the experiences of the last years, we can change this sentence as far as it deals with the problem of government and say, instead,

Between the period of the democratic state run on purely bourgeois lines and that run on purely proletarian lines comes a period of transition from one into the other. A political transition period corresponds to it, the government of which will, as a rule, take the form of a coalition government.[18]

But, while orthodox and revisionists once again found common ground, the gulf dividing them from the revolutionary faction deepened into an unbridgeable chasm. Socialism and communism parted ways and became irreconcilable enemies. The story of this schism is too long and complicated to be told here. Let us only note one curious thing. Both camps of the formerly united Marxist movement hurled a great number and variety of accusations against each other. But the bitterest reproach, perhaps, and one which was to be repeated again and again by both sides alike, was that the other side, by refusing a compromise, had *broken the unity of the world proletariat.* As if that unity had ever existed in fact!

Chapter Seven

Conclusion

Vaguely sensing that something has gone astray in modern life but also strongly convinced that he lacks the power to right whatever is wrong (even if it were possible to discover what is wrong), the individual lives in a sort of eternal adolescent uneasiness. Leo Lowenthal and Norbert Guterman

Superstition cannot be fought with rational means alone, if it is not simultaneously fought with the force of a new faith. Courage, logic, and honest ideals belong together. True, one can fight with pertinent and correct analysis; but one can win victories only if something else goes with it: the voice of an intensive, winning, cheerful, and wrathful belief in the truth, the goodness, and the beauty of one's own cause, the cause of humanity. Joachim Schumacher

The study of Marxism is important on at least three counts. For any social scientist and, perhaps, also for philosophers, Marxism is of interest as a nineteenth-century precursor and pioneer of modern theories. In its Leninist form, moreover, Marxian socialism is perhaps the most important, and to many the most disturbing, *idée-force* in the world today; hence it is of interest to the historian and political scientist studying contemporary problems and to policymakers who seek to grapple with them. Finally, for the student of ideology, the disintegration of Marxism, and its implications, dramatize certain recurrent problems of ideological orientation that are faced by everyone.

For the social scientist in general, Marxism is an important milestone in the development of Western social thought.

Curiously enough, however, it can be considered a milestone only in retrospect. To an amazing extent, the thought of Marx was in vain; his theories were neglected for decades and did not contribute directly to the development of later conceptual schemes. The reason for this may, perhaps, be found primarily in the fact that Marxian sociology was intimately wedded to a political movement and that its truths were often propounded dogmatically and with considerable exaggeration. Hence everything in it that is today considered valid had to be discovered anew by others, and without any connecting links to Marx.

It is perhaps presumptuous to attempt a summary critique of historical materialism here. Enough has been said about the economic interpretation and the limits of its validity. It might be well to emphasize one major source of errors: that is, the narrow cultural bias of Marxism which tends to relate all past history and present politics to the writer's own particular environment. In line with a traditional fallacy of Western historiography, Marx saw history essentially as an unbroken chain of steps that led straight toward industrial capitalism and the proletarian revolution. Similarly, Lenin and his followers came to see all contemporary developments in terms of their own experience in the Russian revolution. In the case of the Russian communists, this may have been due to a peculiar dogmatism that is partly a Marxist trait and partly a product of Russian conditions. In the case of Marx, the root of the fallacy probably lies in the rigidities of his economic interpretation, which has its decided advantages when a specific event or a specific society are to be analyzed, but which turns into a methodological straightjacket when the attempt is made to find a common denominator for all of man's history. On a level as broad as that it still seems more scientific to take recourse to a more impressionistic eclecticism.

The case of dialectics is somewhat more difficult to state. As far as it is the doctrine of the unity of theory and practice, of social science and political attitude, it poses an ideological problem which we shall discuss below. For the rest, we are probably close to an understanding of dialectics if we repeat that it is an abortive attempt to express modern insights by obsolete philosophical concepts. In effect, many of its truths have been accepted by bourgeois social science, and could be accepted more readily because they were expressed without the incrustations of Hegelian jargon.

Despite the failures of Marxism we must not forget the pioneer character of this grand attempt to unite all the philosophical, scientific, and moral strands of the Victorian age into one vast system with almost universal scope. The low degree of scientific accuracy which marks numerous aspects of Marxism, the fuzziness and ambiguity of many of its concepts, cannot detract from the impressive majesty of its thought structure, just as the incomparable vision of Freud cannot appear less brilliant by the countless corrections to which his ideas have been subjected.

It is precisely this attempt at an over-all synthesis of nineteenth-century moral and scientific thought which has given Marxism such a powerful influence over intellectuals and vast social movements throughout the world and has made it one of the most significant rallying cries of our century. To explain the attractiveness of Marxism as an ideology is the task of the student of contemporary history. One of the secrets of this success is the close tie of Marxist analysis to a value orientation: radical criticism of bourgeois society, of America, of colonialism, of every system of exploitation and inequality. Marxism further expresses the yearning of backward societies for a place in the sun, of underprivileged minorities for equal treatment, of manual workers for a place of respect in their social system. It proclaims the cause of progress in areas and in social strata where this word has not yet acquired a hollow sound. It brings to the underprivileged the hope and the conviction that they will catch up with, and overtake, those who are on top today; that the last shall be the first, and not in a paradise beyond, but on this earth and in the near future. Moreover, Marxism boasts that it extends to social processes that scientific technology which has so impressively changed the material aspects of life of proletarians and backward nations. It can all the more easily lay an exclusive claim to scientific validity in social thought because it has often been the first or only one to tackle problems which are crucial to the strata on which it relies.

For troubled intellectuals everywhere, its chief attraction lies in the proclaimed unity of theory and practice, in the attempt to find a broad synthesis of radical criticism, sober science, and a belief in progress. However much its proponents may denounce religion, Marxism as an ideology endeavors to satisfy all the religious urges in men, and the claim to be scientific can be seen as a necessary prerequisite in the modern age, without which men would not even be religious. Marxism is a doctrine of salvation and damnation, and some of the same fears and hopes which drew men into the fold of religions in the past now cause them to join this movement.[1]

We have spoken of the disintegration of this ideology. The grand synthesis fell apart, not only because of its inherent logical inconsistencies, but also because the psychological dispositions which made it seem plausible disappeared with the deceptive harmony of the Victorian age. It must be clearly understood by the reader that this falling apart of Marxism does not by any means indicate its disappearance or even its decay. On the contrary, many heirs of Marx and Engels have been and are still doing extremely fruitful work as social scientists. In that sense, the disintegration of Marxism can be seen as a blossoming and flourishing of Marx's ideas into many different directions. And yet, the unity of the essential elements which we have singled out as the basic components of Marxism has been destroyed. The very ruins of this imposing intellectual edifice, however, confront us with one of the thorniest and most painful questions of all; the problem of our attitude to contemporary events, and its relationship to social science.

The concept of the unity of theory and practice makes us aware of the inseparable connection between social science, political attitude, and action. The social scientist cannot help being a citizen, and the question is whether the citizen and the scientist can dwell in the same individual without influencing each other, whether part of the citizen can encapsulate itself into scientific detachment without either the citizen's decisions or the scientist's findings being affected thereby. Is pure science inevitably conservative or inevitably revolutionary? Both assertions have been made. And how would the answer to this affect our attitude to pure science? Does maximal detachment from politics leave the social scientist in a vacuum and render his findings worthless? Or should we, as citizens, condemn the social scientist who seeks detachment as one who tries to escape from his responsibilities? Conversely, the question as to how various political attitudes affect and distort the social scientist's findings cannot be dismissed lightly. On the contrary, once these problems are thought through, a chasm seems to open which divides social scientists according to their explicit or implicit, conscious or unconscious, political attitudes, preventing them forever from tackling the same problems, coming to similar conclusions, or even speaking the same language. This is the end of the notion that there can be any detached, dispassionate, pure social science; everything turns into ideology.

Furthermore, the breakdown of Marxist optimism poses a problem for all those who either believe in progress or aim to work for the improvement of man's conditions. Whatever the definition of progress or improvement, it was possible, a hundred years ago, to have a rather uncomplicated attitude of round approval toward the idea; the road to progress was either seen as a cumulative process in which achievement would be heaped upon achievement, or as a millennial act which would, with one stroke, liberate all that was good and desirable, or even a combination of both. The latter notion not only betrays unbounded impatience with the painful and wasteful process of history; it also implies the conviction that all the ideals which are part of the humanist tradition depend on each other for their realization. In the really ideal society there can be no hierarchy of values, no difference in the degree to which various ideals have been achieved; instead, all parts of the whole must be perfect in themselves for the whole to be perfect, and not a single part can be perfect without every other part having been brought to perfection. As far as the values of the Western tradition are concerned, Marxism asserts that it must be all or nothing. "A truly human ethics," wrote Engels "standing above class contradictions and above the memory of them, will be possible only on a stage of development in society which has not only overcome the antimony of classes, but has also forgotten it for the practice of life." [2] Implicit in this is the opinion that all features of alienation must have withered away before man's inherent goodness and rationality can flourish. Sensing this, the followers of Marx and Engels have cast bitter moral aspersions on anyone who would be satisfied with less than this paradise on earth.

With their insistence that optimism and social science go together, Marx and Engels were typical representatives of the nineteenth century. The conviction that science could demonstrate the inevitability of progress was as typical of early liberalism as it is of Marxism. And, just as the liberal dream has given way to a much more stoical attitude, which is, perhaps, best expressed in existentialist thought, so the Marxist dreams of the speedy recuperation of paradise in this world were disappointed. The image of the proletariat as the messianic force of salvation has faded away. We have no faith in any class, group, or nation, to deliver us from evil. The earthly forces of salvation have gone the same way which the divine forces did, a century or two earlier. This is, therefore, indeed the age of longing, the age which has brought about that mental disposition which Lowenthal and Guterman have described as *Weltschmerz in perpetuum*.

Both liberalism and Marxism have been forced to make practical, realistic adjustments to this age of disappointment, an age and a world in which substantial progress in one area can be achieved only at the price of serious reverses in another. It used to be so safe and so easy to be a radical. Since all roads inevitably seemed to lead to the good society, no baffling problems of ends versus means presented themselves. To be a radical, or a liberal, did not require sacrificing any moral or aesthetic values whatsoever. In contrast, the breakdown of the unity of theory and practice means that painful choices have to be made. If the pessimistic appraisal of reality be correct, then the Marxian socialist must choose between democracy, together with the preservation of the social *status quo*, on the one hand, and socialism, which according to his analysis can be achieved only through tyrannical means, on the other. In every other field of activity, moral man in an immoral world faces similar excruciating choices. In order to realize any one set of values even partially, another set of values must be sacrificed. But all values are integral parts of the same Western tradition; so that those who are steeped in this tradition are morally torn to pieces by the necessity of having to make a choice, by the need for establishing an order of priorities in their ideals. Any such hierarchy of ideals, any choice between courses that might lead to the Good Society must be denounced as a reflection of personal or group biases. Whatever is done can be condemned by the standards of the universally accepted morality. In this dilemma, the notion of progress threatens to lose all meaning, or else the individual's attitude to progress must become extremely ambivalent.

We are forced, therefore, to turn against the broad and all-inclusive humanist morality, as unrealistic, utopian, and thoroughly otherworldly, an ethic which is honored only in the breach while being used to cloak unmoral or amoral deeds. The very fact that Marx attempted to establish his universal ethic by scientific deduction shows his awareness that there is no fool-proof justification, either otherworldly or philosophical, for such a universal ethic. Recognizing this, one might attempt to substitute a pragmatic morality, free from *a priori* judgments or revealed truths. But this would either be conceived as a universally applicable moral code and therefore be just as unrealistic; or else it would lead straight into moral relativism, which is a denial of all morality, that is, the recognition that life in a divided, competitive, and scarcity-ridden world is a struggle of all against all. This is exactly the development which took place, with modifications, in both liberalism and Marxism.

Nor does the assertion stand up that moral systems, however utopian, do serve as checks against barbarian excesses. Neither Christianity nor humanist ideals succeeded in preventing the bestialities of Auschwitz and Buchenwald. Indeed, rather, it often seems that the existence of moral sentiments or moral convictions permit inhumanities of this sort; they serve as some sort of otherworldliness which lulls us into the pleasant belief that, somehow, somewhere, the perpetrators will be punished. Thus moral convictions allow us to bear the evil against which, without these, we might rebel. And there is surely no need to point out that moral convictions have always supplied direct justification for the perpetration of inhumanities. In this sense, the very comprehensiveness of the aims of secular humanism, not only in its Marxist form, condones totalitarianism. Christian writers, confident of the good life beyond, have, therefore, warned against all grand inquisitors who want to work for the good life on this earth. Yet, if we are satisfied with less than what seems possible of achievement, are we not smugly condoning the existing inhumanities from the very beginning?

These are some of the tormenting doubts that flow from the disintegration of Marxism. They are dramatized by this disintegration precisely because the theory of Marx was, perhaps, the last attempt to combine absolute, radical, grandiose humanistic ideals with the most hardheaded and coldblooded realism. Both this idealism and this realism are part of our intellectual tradition. In its abortive attempt to drive both strands to their logical conclusion and then combine them in a grand synthesis, Marxism has thrown a light on the shaky foundations of this tradition and thus compels us to explore the frontiers of our philosophy.

NOTES

BIBLIOGRAPHY

INDEX

Notes

With the exception of Lenin's works, which are cited in their Russian-language edition, an attempt has been made, whenever possible, to cite English-language editions of all works used. At the same time the author has felt free to substitute his own translation of the original for the wording of the edition cited.

Introduction, 1954

1. The literary relationship between the two friends might be summarized in the following manner. (a) Engels was an all-important influence in forming Marx's economc ideas, and Marx acknowledged this debt by frequent references, in *Das Kapital*, to the two pertinent works of his friend, *Die Lage der arbeitenden Klasse in England*, and *Umrisse zu einer Kritik der Nationalökonomie*. (b) The early years of their acquaintance saw a very intimate collaboration which yielded a number of joint works, the most important of them being *Die deutsche Ideologie*. In some form, this collaboration lasted well beyond the death of Marx. Engels was far more than a mere editor in bringing out volumes II and III of *Das Kapital*. While Marx was alive, an intensive interchange of ideas took place which again was so intimate that even some of the works published under the name of Marx must be characterized either as joint works or as the works of Engels. (c) Engels continued to be an author in his own right and must be considered a keen analyst of the political events of his day; he is particularly successful as an analyst of military developments. His later ventures into philosophy and natural history, which are partly popularizations of Marxist ideas, partly attempts to apply Marxism to nonhistorical phenomena, are of little or no relevance to the present work.

2. Karl Korsch, *Karl Marx* (New York: John Wiley & Sons, 1938), p. 12.

3. For an exposition of some of these difficulties, see Gregory Grossman, "Scarce Capital and Soviet Doctrine," in *The Quarterly Journal of Economics*, vol. LXVII (August, 1953), no. 3, pp. 311–343.

Chapter 1: The Marxist Contribution to Contemporary Social Science

1. Karl Marx, *Capital* (Chicago: Charles H. Kerr & Co., revised edition by Ernest Untermann; vol. I, 1906; vol. II, 1933; vol. III, 1909), I, 22–24. This is a quotation by Marx in the Preface to the second edition from a book review of the first edition of *Das Kapital*, to which he adds the following comment: "Whilst the writer pictures what he takes to be actually my method, in this striking and (as far as concerns my own application of it) generous way, what else is he picturing but the dialectical method?"

2. Stated in this general form, this idea is accepted as commonplace by a whole number of social scientists entirely outside the Marxist camp, particularly anthropologists.

3. *Capital*, III, 954–955. Cf. also Ernst Lewalter, "Wissenssoziologie und Marxismus," *Archiv für Sozialwissenschaft und Sozialpolitik*, vol. 64, no. 1, p. 83, and *passim*.

4. Friedrich Engels, *Ludwig Feuerbach and the Outcome of Classical German Philosophy* (New York: International Publishers, 1941), p. 31.

5. Karl Marx and Friedrich Engels, *Die heilige Familie*, in Marx und Engels, *Historisch-kritische Gesamtausgabe*, sec. I, vol. 3, p. 294.

6. Karl Marx and Friedrich Engels, *Die deutsche Ideologie*, in *Gesamtausgabe*, sec. I, vol. 5, p. 357. Cf. also *ibid.*, p. 9.

7. Karl Marx, *The Eighteenth Brumaire of Louis Bonaparte* (New York: International Publishers, 1935), p. 13.

8. Cf. another early statement of this position: "In real history, those theoreticians who consider *power* as the basis of law are in direct contrast to those who see *will* as the basis of law. . . . When power is assumed to be the basis of law, as is done by Hobbes etc., then law, legislation, etc., are only symptoms, the expression of *different* relationships on which the power of the state rests. The material life of the individuals, which is in no wise dependent on their mere "will," their mode of production, and their form of traffic [(*Verkehrsform*); this term was later generally replaced by the term, relations of production], which condition each other reciprocally, is the real basis of the state, and remains the basis in all stages in which the division of labor and private property are still necessary, quite independently of the individuals' *will*. These real relationships are not at all created by the power of the state; instead, they are the force that creates the latter. The power of the individuals ruling under these conditions has to constitute itself as *state;* but even without this they have to give their will, determined by these conditions, a general expression as the will of the state, as law — an expression the content of which is al-

ways given by the conditions of this class, as our private and criminal law demonstrate in the clearest fashion."

9. Cf. Marx and Engels, *Die heilige Familie*, p. 298.

10. Marx, with obvious approval, quotes Vico as saying that "human history differs from natural history in this, that we have made the former, but not the latter." *Capital*, I, 406.

11. *Ludwig Feuerbach*, p. 30.

12. Marx and Engels, *Die deutsche Ideologie*, p. 27.

13. Marx, Third "Thesis on Feuerbach" in Marx and Engels, *Gesamtausgabe*, sec. I, vol. 5.

14. For a Marxist's attempt to describe the relationship between Marxism and the "so-called 'sociology' of Comte, Spencer, and their followers," see the first chapter of Korsch, *Karl Marx*.

15. *Die deutsche Ideologie*.

16. V. Adoratsky, *Dialectical Materialism* (New York: International Publishers, 1934), p. 62.

17. *Ludwig Feuerbach*, p. 67. The implication of this attack on philosophy is that philosophy and science are sharply contrasted, presumably on the ground that the latter consists of empirically verifiable statements (hypotheses) whereas the former does not. And whatever "philosophic" statements Engels propounded, he was always eager to point out that they were derived from empirical observation, different from other scientific statements only in the degree of their abstractness, and that they were verifiable. However abstract his statements about the nature of reality, he constantly repeated that they were science and — by implication — not philosophy.

The trouble is, however, that substantial bits of Engels' generalization would by no means stand up to empirical verification, and that his own tests of verification are often inadequate.

18. *Die deutsche Ideologie*, p. 16.

19. *Ludwig Feuerbach*, p. 56.

20. For a discussion of human nature to which Marx and Engels might have subscribed wholeheartedly, even though it was not written by one of their followers, see Julian Huxley, "The Uniqueness of Man," in his *Man Stands Alone* (New York: Harper and Brothers, 1941).

21. Marx defines labor as "the exercize of human capabilities, both mental and physical, for the production of use-values." *Capital*, I, 186.

22. *Die deutsche Ideologie*, p. 10. See also the following statement: "A spider conducts operations that resemble those of a weaver, and a bee puts to shame many an architect in the construction of her cells. But what distinguishes the worst architect from the best of bees is this, that the architect raises his structure in imagination before he erects it in reality" *Capital*, I, 198. For a more extended treatment of this aspect of Marxism, see Vernon Venable, *Human Nature, the Marxist View* (New York: Alfred Knopf, 1945). For a non-Marxist's concept of the relation

between personality and culture which is strikingly similar to the Marxist view, see Gardner Murphy, "The Relationship of Culture and Personality," in *Culture and Personality*, proceedings of an interdisciplinary conference held under the auspices of the Viking Fund, November 7 and 8, 1947 (New York: Viking Fund, 1949), pp. 13–27.

23. Karl Marx, *Zur Kritik der politischen (Ökonomie* 4th ed.; Stuttgart: Verlag von J. H. W. Dietz, Nachf., 1919), pp. xviii–xix.

24. *Ibid.*, p. 273.

25. *Ibid.*, pp. xxxii–xxxiii.

26. Friedrich Engels, *Ursprung der Familie, des Privateigentums, und des Staates* (Züruch: Schweizerische Genossenschaftsbuchdruckerei, 1884), p. 117. This passage recalls a case told by Darwin of a forest, parts of which showed that they had once been cleared and made into a farm. Yet the farm had been deserted long ago, and where it had stood the very same kinds of plants were now growing that made up the rest of the forest. An iron necessity similar to that described by Engels had made for the survival of exactly the same flora which in the remainder of the forest had shown that it was best adapted for the conditions of nature prevailing in that place.

27. Sometimes this concept is used interchangeably with "means of production," which is equally ambiguous, as the following passage might illustrate: "If we examine the whole process from the point of view of its result, the product, it is plain that both the instruments and the subject of labor are means of production . . ." *Capital*, I, 201. This sentence is rendered even more opaque by a footnote which we forego quoting.

28. Marx, letter to Annenkov, 28 December 1846, in *The Poverty of Philosophy* (New York: International Publishers, 1939), p. 152. (Italics added.)

29. John H. Hallowell, *Main Currents in Modern Political Thought* (New York: Henry Holt, 1950), ch. 12, note 15, p. 723.

30. *Poverty of Philosophy*, p. 97.

31. *Ibid.*

32. Marx, *A Contribution to the Critique of Political Economy*, Preface, p. 11.

33. *Poverty of Philosophy*, p. 113.

34. "Relics of by-gone instruments of labor possess the same importance for the investigation of extinct economical forms of society, as do fossil bones for the determination of extinct species of animals. It is not the articles made, but how they are made, and by what instruments, that enables us to distinguish different economical epochs. Instruments of labour not only supply a standard of the degree of development to which human labour has attained, but they are also *indicators* of the social conditions under which that labour is carried on." *Capital*, I, 200.

"Technology *discloses* man's mode of dealing with Nature, the process of production by which he sustains his life, and thereby also *lays bare* the mode of formation of his social relations, and of the mental conceptions that flow from them. Every history of religion, even, that fails to take account of this material basis, is uncritical." *Ibid.*, p. 406. (Italics added.)

35. Marx and Engels referred to this control over the essential means of production and communication as "property." Hence Marx could assert that ". . . forms of property . . . form the solid basis of the political organization, and . . . must be continually reproduced in order that the political organization may endure." *Capital*, III, 701. In choosing this word, property, they did not realize how much trouble they were thereby causing their doctrinaire followers. For property is, clearly, not the only possible way in which a ruling class can wield decisive control over the means of production. The feudal world did not know the institution of property in the modern sense of the word; nor does this institution exist in Soviet society. Yet only Soviet ideologists would conclude from this that their society is without an exploiter class and exploited classes.

36. Cf., for instance, *Die deutsche Ideologie*, p. 15.

37. Quoted by Ernst Drahn, *Friedrich Engels: ein Lebensbild zu seinem 100. Geburtstage* (Wien: Verlag Arbeiter-Buchhandlung, 1920), p. 122.

38. *Capital*, I, 83.

39. At the same time it is interesting to note the keen attention with which leading Marxists like Engels, Luxemburg, Plekhanov, Kautsky, and others, followed the development of modern anthropology.

40. Though he is interested foremost in the *social relations* pertaining to different economic systems.-Cf. above, p. 21.

41. Cf. pp. 29–30.

42. *Capital*, III, 919.

43. Friedrich Engels, letter to Bloch, 21 September 1890. Cf. also his letter to Heinz Starkenburg, 25 January 1894. In Karl Marx and Friedrich Engels, *Selected Correspondence* (New York: International Publishers, 1934), XXIX, 475, 516.

44. Eduard Bernstein, *Evolutionary Socialism* (London: Independent Labour Party, 1909), p. 12.

45. *Die deutsche Ideologie*, p. 27.

46. That Lenin preferred functional thinking to cause-and-effect thinking appears from a suggestion he made in reference to a proposed draft for a Party program: "In Paragraph (A) II, instead of the words: 'The uninterrupted improvement of technology leads to the increasing replacement of small production by large-scale production,' put the following sentence: 'Uninterrupted, the improvement of technology advances, large-scale production develops stronger and stronger, more and more small production is forced out or goes to its ruin.'" To put this into cause-and-effect terms, he adds, would be "against logic," meaning, against the logic of events. For, he concludes, it is all the same process, in which everything is at once

cause and effect, and causal thinking would lead nowhere." "Materialy k vyrabotke programmy RSDRP" in Lenin, *Sochineniia*, 2nd ed.; vol. V, pp. 17–20.

47. Talcott Parsons, "The Present Position and Prospects of Systematic Theory in Sociology," in *20th Century Sociology* (ed. Gurvitch, Georgii, and Moore; New York: Philosophical Library, 1945), p. 48. Cf. also the following statement: "The most essential condition of successful dynamic analysis is continual and systematic reference of every problem to the state of the system as a whole." *Ibid.*, p. 47.

48. *Die deutsche Ideologie*, p. 16. Cf. Lenin: "Up to now the social scientists have taken pains to distinguish within the complex pattern of social phenomena between *important* and *unimportant* features (here we have the roots of subjectivism in social science), and they have not succeeded in finding an objective criterion for such a separation. Materialism has given us a completely objective criterion by taking the 'relation of production' as the structure of society." "Chto takoe druz'ia naroda?" in Lenin, *Sobranie Sochinenii*, ed. I, vol. I, p. 71.

49. *Zur Kritik der politischen Ökonomie*, 4th ed., Vorwort, p. xxiv. It is interesting to note that a famous contemporary of Marx and Engels, Charles Darwin, was able to express the functional approach far more clearly. Cf., for instance, the following passages:

"When one part varies, and the variations are accumulated through natural selection, other modifications, often of the most unexpected nature, will ensue." *Origin of Species* (New York: American Home Library, 1902), p. 128.

". . . the structure of every organic being is related, in the most essential yet often hidden manner, to that of all the other organic beings with which it comes into competition for food or residence, or from which it has to escape, or on which it preys." *Ibid.*, p. 117.

"When we travel southward and see a species decreasing in numbers, we may feel sure that the cause lies quite as much in other species being favored as in this one being hurt." *Ibid.*, p. 108.

In turn, Darwin's manner of argument greatly influenced Engels, whose own writings on evolution — attempts to demonstrate dialectical relationships in nature — employ very similar ways of argument and description. Cf. particularly "Die Rolle der Arbeit in der Menschwerdung des Affen," in Otto Jenssen (ed.), *Marxismus und Naturwissenschaft* (Sonderausgabe; Berlin: Verlagsgesellschaft des allgemeinen deutschen Gewerkschaftsbundes, m.b.H., 1925).

50. It must be pointed out once more that the Marxist tradition itself is strongly wedded to mechanistic thought. So far, we have attempted to prove that the Marxist method means an abandonment of cause-and-effect thinking. But this is but the interpretation of an outsider, which might not get the assent of many Marxists. The very terminology in which the functional theory of Marxism is couched betrays the deep roots with which

it is planted in the soil of causal thought. The very nature of the functional relationship in which both variables are "both cause and effect" of each other — indeed a phrase which shows how clumsily Marxist theory was groping for a terminology that might serve it in thinking about complex processes in terms other that causal chains.

Another striking instance of mechanistic thinking is the "reflection" theory of knowledge, according to which ideas are reflections of reality — a very Cartesian conception which is discussed briefly in p. 70. Cf. also note 2, ch. 3.

51. Cf. Lenin: "The idea of historic necessity does not in the least undermine the role of personalities in history; history is all composed of the activities of persons, who are indubitable agents. The real question arising in an appraisal of the social activities of persons is: In what conditions are these actions guaranteed success? Where is the guarantee that this action will not remain a solitary deed drowned in a sea of contrary activities?" "Chto takoe druz'ia naroda?"

52. This, at least, would be the reasonable stand to take. We shall see that Marx and Engels, not content with this position, tended to think that the development of a *functional* superstructure over the economic substructure is inevitable, in the long run.

53. *Capital*, I, 94. (Italics added.)

54. An illustration of the unnecessary difficulties created by the conversion of logic into empirical abstractions (and vice versa) is furnished by the futile attempts currently made by Soviet philosophers to distinguish clearly between "formal logic" i.e., the nonempirical logic accepted by most other philosophies, and "dialectical logic" which is both logic and empirical knowledge.

55. Friedrich Engels, *Herr Eugen Dühring's Revolution in Science* (*Anti-Dühring*) (New York: International Publishers, 1939).

56. Cf. Eduard Heimann, *Freedom and Order* (New York: Charles Scribner's Sons, 1947), *passim*.

57. This is done by Karl Kautsky, *Der politische Massenstreik* (Berlin: Paul Singer Verlag, 1914), p. 9.

Chapter 2: Marx as a Radical Critic of Civilization

1. *Marx and Lenin: the Science of Revolution* (New York: Albert and Charles Boni, 1927), p. 262.

2. Cf. Lenin, "Chto takoe druz'ia naroda?," in *Sochineniia*, 2nd ed., vol. I, p. 78.

3. Marx, letter to Ruge, September 1843, in Marx and Engels, *Über historischen Materialismus* (Berlin: Internationaler Arbeiter Verlag, G.M.B.H., 1930), pt. I, p. 14.

4. *Die deutsche Ideologie*, p. 45.

5. Lenin, "Krizis men'shevizma," in *Sochineniia*, 2nd ed., vol. X, p. 186.

6. Karl Marx, "Zur Kritik der Hegelschen Rechtsphilosophie," in Marx and Engels, *Der historische Materialismus; Die Frühschriften* (Leipzig: Alfred Kröner Verlag, 1932), I, 272. (Italics added.)

7. Thus, for instance, Marx expressed the wish that someone write a "critical history of technology." *Capital*, I, 406. See also the second passage quoted in note 34, chapter 1.

8. *Ludwig Feuerbach*, p. 11.

9. *Ibid.*, p. 12. (Italics added.)

10. The word *conservatism* may lead to a misunderstanding. Certainly, the Soviet regime has not shown any intention to cease harassing its people into building an entirely new way of life, whether they wish it or not. Certainly, it treats its society as an experimental workshop of human relations, in which institutions can be abolished as quickly and as thoroughly as they were created. In this sense the Soviet regime has remained profoundly revolutionary.

But it has also devised an elaborate machinery for the purpose of securing its own political stability; it has shown itself ready to sacrifice socialist ideals and revolutionary goals for the sake of such stability; it has restored and strengthened institutions and habits which are generally regarded as reactionary and were once denounced as such; finally, it has transformed its ideological heritage into an apologetic theory of state. All these features give the Soviet regime a decidedly conservative cast.

11. The futuristic fallacy of Marxist dialectics has been explored by Karl Popper, *The Open Society and Its Enemies*, vol. II.

12. *Ludwig Feuerbach*, p. 11. (Italics added.)

13. For a fuller treatment of these and other aspects of Leninism see the author's *Leninism* (Cambridge: Harvard University Press, 1957).

14. "Doklad ob ob"edinitel'nom s"ezde RSDRP (pis'mo k peterburgskim rabochim)" in *Sochineniia*, ed. 2, vol. IX, p. 201.

15. *Anti-Dühring*, p. 158.

16. *Die deutsche Ideologie*, p. 11.

17. It must be pointed out once more that modern anthropology has not confirmed either the work ·of Morgan or the interpretation which Engels made on its basis. Marxists, like Rosa Luxemburg and George Plekhanov, who had familiarized themselves with contemporary anthropological literature, have shown little interest in this work of Engels.

18. Friedrich Engels, *The Origins of the Family, Private Property, and the State* (Moscow: Foreign Languages Publishing House, 1948), pp. 247-248. See also *Capital*, I, 56: "If the laborer wants all his time to produce the necessary means of subsistence for himself and his race, he has no time left in which to work gratis for others.

"Without a certain degree of productiveness in his labor, he has no such superfluous time at his disposal; without such superfluous time, no surplus-labor, and therefore no capitalists, no slave-owners, no feudal lords, in one word, no class of large proprietors."

19. *The Origins of the Family*, p. 160.

20. The book in which Engels develops his theory, according to which the division of labor, and all its consequences, grew out of tribal societies, is so well known that it might be worth pointing out that Marx, in an earlier work, had traced the division of labor to the family, not the tribe. See *Capital*, I, 386.

21. *Poverty of Philosophy*, p. 53.

22. Marx began his first literary activities as a radical democrat. In democracy, he wrote, the general will of the real people becomes incarnate in the actions of the state. See *Kritik der Hegelschen Staatsphilosophie*, in Marx and Engels, *Frühschriften*, I, 54–55. Freedom, he held, is the identity of private interest with the interests of the state and the community. In case of collisions between the two it is, formally, the state which decides between special interests and the interests of the community; and the state makes such decisions in the name of the community. In reality, however — and here his criticism sets in — the state has, so far, always been the creation of special interests. (*Ibid.*, pp. 20–22.) Thus the political ideal of the young Marx is posited clearly: The state must be liberated from domination by special interests, if it is to be transformed into an instrument of the people, into a true democracy. As soon as this is accomplished, however, the state will itself have become superfluous. Once the general will has found it possible to overcome the restrictions of outworn institutions, the state can be allowed to wither away. Democracy in the fullest meaning of the word means the end of the state. (*Ibid.*, p. 56.)

23. *Origins of the Family*, p. 241. See also *Anti-Dühring*, Part 2, ch. iv.

24. *Ludwig Feuerbach*, pp. 60–61. This means that, according to the Marxist theory, all struggles between classes over policies must become political conflicts. Kautsky explained this once by pointing out that economic purpose organizations serve primarily the common *personal* interests of their members. Only the struggle for control of the state turns men's minds from momentary objectives to all-embracing aims. Thus, not only does class struggle manifest itself as political struggle, but, more important, only the political struggle creates a real class interest. Only a class which wages a political struggle can be said to be waging class struggle. See *Die Klassengegensätze im Zeitalter der französischen Revolution* (Stuttgart: Dietz, 1919), p. 10. This insistence that the class struggle is a political struggle, not a struggle over economic benefits, is the foundation for Lenin's fight against what he considered to be the heresies of economism and trade-unionism, i.e., an emphasis on the efforts of the working class to improve its lot pending the overthrow of the capitalist system by the proletarian revolution.

25. *Origins of the Family*, pp. 241–242.

26. *Ibid.*, p. 168.

27. Note that the concept of lag is not the exclusive property of Marxism. Thus Alfred Weber views history as a process in which civilizational change tends to outrun cultural change; according to Ogburn, material factors change more rapidly than nonmaterial; and in Scheler's theories, "artificial" types of knowledge change faster than less artificial types. Cf. Merton, "The Sociology of Knowledge," in Gurvich, Georgii, and Moore (eds.), *Twentieth Century Sociology* (New York: Philosophy Library, 1945), pp. 383–384. Many of these ideas can probably be traced either to the romantics or to Marx.

28. Quoted in Georg Lukács, *Geschichte und Klassenbewusstzein* (Wien: Malik-Verlag, 1923), p. 255. Cf. Engels, *Origin of the Family*, p. 160: "In the long run no society can retain mastery over its own production and control over the social effects of the process of its production."

29. Preface to *Critique of Political Economy*. For this reason Marxism refuses to deal with any particular aspect of human culture out of context with the history of culture as such. Marxists will not, for instance, write a history of law or any of its aspects, a history of painting, government, or fashion, except for the purpose of *illustrating* and *highlighting* the history of the social structure as a whole. These particular histories are, then, seen only as a running comment on the history of society as such.

30. *Poverty of Philosophy*, p. 30.

31. For an interesting attempt to write the history of the "first bourgeois revolution" out of which commodity production emerged, see Karl August Wittfogel, *Geschichte der bürgerlichen Gesellschaft von ihren Anfängen bis zur Schwelle der französischen Revolution* (Wien: Malik-Verlag, 1924). This "first bourgeois revolution," which Wittfogel places, roughly, in the twelfth century, must not be confused with the beginnings of capitalism, which Marx places in the sixteenth century.

32. Here and in the following pages, I am leaning heavily on the lucid exposition of Paul Sweezy, *The Theory of Capitalist Development* (New York: Oxford University Press, 1942).

33. *Selected Correspondence of Marx and Engels* (New York: International Publishers, 1934), p. 246.

34. G. D. H. Cole cogently expresses Marx's intentions: "Ricardo had, indeed, admitted that certain natural objects might possess a value, by which he meant a price, by virtue of their natural scarcity. But Marx, who does not mean 'price' when he says 'value,' is under no necessity to admit this exception. Value consists, *in his definition*, of that which man adds by his efforts to what is conferred upon him by nature." *What Marx Really Meant* (New York: Alfred A. Knopf, 1934), pp. 210–211. (Italics added.)

35. *Capital*, III, 214. Quoted in Paul Sweezy, *The Theory of Capitalist Development*, p. 51.

36. For a definition of fetishism, see pp. 21–22.

37. The following statement illustrates this point emphatically: "Money is not a thing, it is a social relation . . . this relation is a link and, as such, closely connected with a whole chain of other economic relations . . . this relation corresponds to a definite mode of production neither more nor less than does individual exchange." *Poverty of Philosophy*, p. 68. Cf. also, *Capital*, I, 55: ". . . the value of commodities has a purely social reality . . . value can only manifest itself in the social relation of commodity to commodity . . ."

38. Marx's acceptance of the concepts of classical economists is emphasized by no one so much as Marx himself; witness the countless references, in his economic writings, to their works. It may, however, be somewhat misleading to say that he disagreed with them only over the major goals of their research. Even in quoting them, and in praising their writings, he tried to show again and again that their bourgeois attitude inevitably prevented them from perceiving the inner coherence of their own economic system. Hence, in his opinion, they could perceive problems and express them in their concepts, but they could not solve them; they provided theoretical tools, but were unable to carry out the job of thorough analysis. Lukács, in a boastful tone, has this to say about it: ". . . the decided superiority of Marxian economics over all its predecessors and successors [*sic*] consists in the fact that, even in the most complex questions where, seemingly, the purest economic . . . categories must be applied, it has worked out a method by which it can formulate the problem in such a manner that behind the "purely economic" categories the classes have become apparent in their processes of development, — those classes which express these economic categories in their social existence." *Lenin, Studie über den Zusammenhang seiner Gedanken* (Wien: Malik-Verlag, 1924), p. 38.

39. At the same time it becomes apparent why this labor theory and most other parts of the "purely economic" concepts of Marx are not required for the essentially sociological theory of Marxism. R. N. Carew Hunt is mistaken when he writes, "It is on this fundamental assumption that . . . wage labor is the sole value-producing agency that the theory stands or falls." *Theory and Practice of Communism* (New York: Macmillan Co. 1951), p. 60. The analysis of class society in which a minority owns the crucial means of production, forcing the majority of nonpropertied to work with these means of production, is really independent of the theory of value, which is no more than an abstract and, perhaps, abstruse expression of this relationship. Cf. Joan Robinson, *Essay on Marxian Economics* (London: Macmillan & Co., 1949), pp. 17–22.

40. *Capital*, I, 189, quoted by Sweezy, *The Theory of Capitalist Development*, pp. 50, 59.

41. Very much like the classical economists, Marx regards the capitalist as nothing more than the man who furnishes capital, and thus disregards the value that might be created by managerial work. It is, in part, this

simplified image which the classical economists had of the entrepreneur which enabled Marx to use their theories as a basis from which to advocate the expropriation of the capitalist class. For, if capital were furnished by "society as a whole," the capitalist would truly be a superfluous man. The same disregard of the complexity of managerial functions explains the bland optimism of Lenin's view of a push-button society in which every cook could take his turn at governing.

42. An investigation of the origins of capitalism therefore must center around the process by which "free labor" became available. This actual birth of capitalism is placed by Marx around the sixteenth century and later. Cf. also Wittfogel, *Geschichte der bürgerlichen Gesellschaft*, pp. 123-125, and Engels, *The Peasant War in Germany* (London: Allen and Unwin, 1927), *passim*. Cf. also, note 44 to this chapter.

43. *Poverty of Philosophy*, p. 31. For an application of these concepts to the contemporary scene, see C. Wright Mills, *White Collar* (New York: Oxford University Press, 1951); Erich Fromm, *Man for Himself* (New York: Rinehart, 1947); and David Riesman, *The Lonely Crowd* (New Haven: Yale University Press, 1950). Fromm speaks of the problems faced by individuals when they find that the world is a market place for personality. Riesman speaks of modern society as a "big salesroom." One of the horrors of this big salesroom is scarcely touched upon by these writers; we mean the growing tendency for this market to be a fixed market, which causes a chronic oversupply of personality, with consequent loss in its value.

44. Marx, after describing the process of capitalist production, points out that the very functioning of this process presupposes an accumulation of capital which is "not the result of the capitalist mode of production, but its starting point." See *Capital*, I, 784. This he calls "primitive accumulation," and its methods, he adds, were "anything but idyllic." On the contrary, they consisted in "conquest, enslavement, robbery, murder, briefly force" (*Ibid.*, p. 875), for violence and coercion is required to rob the small property owner of his means of production and transform him into a proletarian. After describing the period of primitive accumulation in horrid detail, Marx comes to the conclusion that ". . . capital comes [into the world] dripping from head to foot, from every pore, with blood and dirt." *Ibid.*, p. 834.

45. *The Poverty of Philosophy*, pp. 46–47. See also the following statements:

"Capital is dead labour, that vampire-like, only lives by sucking living labour and lives the more, the more labour it sucks." *Capital*, I, 257.

"The means of production are at once changed into means for the absorption of the labour of others. It is now no longer the labourer that employs the means of production, but the means of production that employ the labourer. Instead of being consumed by him as material elements of his productive activity, they consume him as the ferment necessary to their own life-process, and the life-process of capital consists only in its move-ment, as value constantly expanding, constantly multiplying itself." *Ibid.*, p. 339.

"In handicrafts and manufacture, the workman makes use of a tool, in the factory, the machine makes use of him. There the movements of the instrument of labour proceed from him, here it is the movements of the machine that he must follow. In manufacture the workmen are parts of a living mechanism. In the factory we have a lifeless mechanism independent of the workman, who becomes its mere living appendage." *Ibid.*, pp. 461–462.

46. Engels, letter to Mehring, 14 July 1893, in Marx and Engels, *Selected Correspondence*, p. 510.

47. Once again the affinity of this theory of ideology to the Freudian theory of resistance to analysis and self-knowledge must be stressed.

48. Engels, *Ludwig Feuerbach*, p. 61.

49. *Die deutsche Ideologie*, p. 215.

50. Marx, "Kritik der Hegelschen Rechtsphilosophie," in Marx and Engels, *Der historische Materialismus, Die Frühschriften*, pp. 17–18.

51. *Ibid.*

Chapter 3: The Faith in Progress

1. In addition, Marx and Engels have always used the word *material-ism* to mean *empiricism*. Engels, for instance, praises Bacon, among others, for the materialism of his method. "According to his theory, the senses are infallible and the source of all knowledge. Science is empirical and consists in the application of a rational method to the sense data. Induction, analy-sis, comparison, observation, experimentation, are the main conditions of a rational method." "Über historischen Materialismus," in *Ludwig Feuerbach*, p. 82. Thus materialism is defined as a view of reality which relies on the sense data, a view of the world "as it enters into the perception of all those who approach it without preconceived idealistic spleens." *Ludwig Feuer-bach*, p. 50.

2. Perhaps Lenin was familiar with Boswell's story that Dr. Johnson once used the same argument when he heard about the philosophic views of Bishop Berkeley. The only difference was that Johnson kicked a stone instead of knocking against a wall.

3. *Die deutsche Ideologie*, p. 357.

4. Malthus held that population increases at a faster rate than the pro-duction of the means for its subsistence. The growing disproportion, he argued, could be corrected only by ever-recurring social and natural catastrophies, which would serve to decrease the population.

5. This profound horror of Malthusianism has persistently blinded

Soviet economists to the very real problem of whether the level of agricultural production in their country will be able, in future years and decades, to support the rapidly growing population. The most diligent reader is not likely to find references to this problem in Soviet literature.

6. *Capital*, I, 709.

7. *Ibid.*, pp. 836–837.

8. *Ibid.*, p. 259. (Italics added.) See also note 24, chapter 2, of the present work.

9. *The Poverty of Philosophy*, p. 147.

10. *Die heilige Familie.*

11. *The Poverty of Philosophy*, p. 146.

12. "Large-scale industry concentrates in one place a crowd of people unknown to one another. Competition divides their interests. But the maintenance of wages, this common interest which they have against their boss, unites them in a common thought of resistance — *Combination*. Thus combination always has a double aim, that of stopping the competition among themselves, in order to bring about a general competition with the capitalist. If the first aim of resistance was merely the maintenance of wages, combinations, at first isolated, constitute themselves into groups . . . and in the face of ever united capital, the maintenance of the association becomes more necessary to them than that of wages . . . the workers sacrifice a good part of their wages in favor of associations which, in the eyes of these economists, are established solely in favor of wages. In this struggle — a veritable civil war — all the elements necessary for a coming battle are united and developed. Once it has reached this point, association takes on a political character.

"Economic conditions had first transformed the mass of the people of the country into workers. The domination of capital has created for this mass a common situation, common interests. This mass is thus already a class as against capital, but not yet for itself. In the struggle, of which we have noted only a few phases, this mass becomes united and constitutes itself as a class for itself. The interests it defends become class interests. But the struggle of class against class is a political struggle." *Ibid.*, p. 145.

13. *Ibid.*, p. 146.

14. *Anti-Dühring*, p. 207.

15. *The Poverty of Philosophy*, p. 55.

16. *Anti-Dühring*, p. 239. This notion of abundance, essential as it is to the Marxian solution of history's problems, can be attacked on empirical grounds. Even Marxist economists recognize to what extent production determines consumption and supply creates a demand that might forever outstrip available supplies. In this case a satisfaction of demand could never be achieved.

It may also be argued that the earth's resources are limited. But as has already been pointed out, no Marxist will accept this argument; so great is his horror of Malthusianism, so convinced is he that man can lick all problems of production.

17. *Civil Government*, book II, ch. XV, par. 173. This includes the products of their labor, labor being the sole title to the appropriation of a product, both in Locke and in Marx. Engels is careful, however, to make the proviso that "the necessity for a fund for social reserve and accumulation would remain and consequently even in that case while the workers as a whole, i.e. *all* would remain in possession and enjoyment of their total product, each separate worker would not enjoy the 'full product of his labor.' " Preface to first German edition of *The Poverty of Philosophy*, p. 19.

18. *Anti-Dühring*, p. 109.

19. See also the following statement: ". . . the historical development of the antagonisms immanent in a given form of production *is the only way* in which that form of production can be dissolved and a new form established." *Capital*, I, 534–535. (Italics added.)

20. "Rech' ob obmane naroda lozungami svobody i ravenstva, 19 May 1919." I. vserossiiskii s"ezd po vneshkol'nomu obrazovaniiu, *Sochineniia*, 2nd ed., vol. XXIV, p. 306.

21. Engels, *Ludwig Feuerbach*, pp. 11–12.

22. In a similar vein, Marx repeats the old observation that abundance prevents men from developing a mastery over nature. Where nature is too lavish with her gifts, she does not impose any necessity on man to develop himself. Capitalism therefore is the natural product of the temperate zone. *Capital*, I, 563.

No statement can be found in the writings of Marx to justify our assertion that lag stimulates the growth of the forces of production. Instead, he tended to picture the forces of production as growing automatically from their own inner laws and coming into conflict with the lag in the superstructure, particularly the relations of ownership, appropriation, and realization. Hence lag was considered to stimulate nothing except revolution. And yet the image of the forces of production growing automatically from their own inner laws is not at all in keeping with the Marxist method that has been outlined in these pages. It would indeed have to be criticized as "undialectical" and as a fetishistic view. It is perfectly legitimate to correct the views of Marx as inconsistently Marxist in this case.

23. Marx praises "the law discovered by Hegel . . . that merely quantitative differences *beyond a certain point* pass into qualitative changes," and illustrates this by reference to "the molecular theory of modern chemistry first scientifically worked out by Laurent and Gerhardt." As Engels explains this, Marx is here alluding to the observation that "by the simply quantitative addition of CH_2 to the molecular formula [!] [in certain carbon compounds] a qualitatively different body is each time formed." *Capital*, I, 338. (Italics added.)

This illustration proves nothing but the meaninglessness of the dialectical phraseology. There is no "certain point" here beyond which a physical transformation "passes into" a chemical transformation. There is no "quantitative" change here at all, except in the formula and, of course, in the composition of the molecule. But "quantitative" changes of molecules are identical with, not a step toward, chemical transformations.

24. *Anti-Dühring*, p. 138.
25. *Ibid.*, p. 145.
26. *Filosofskie Tetradi*, p. 216. Moscow-Leningrad, 1936.
27. "Uspekhi i trudnosti sovetskoi vlasti," in *Sochineniia*, XXIV, 65. Similarly, he condemned the destruction of manorial property by the irate peasants in the revolution of 1905. Destructiveness, he wrote, is often only the result of our failure *to take and hold* the enemy's possessions. Destruction is thus a sign of weakness. It means impotent revenge on the oppressor in lieu of his actual destruction, the taking-over of his institutions, and the building of a new and better society.

Chapter 4: The Unity and Theory of Practice

1. One need not, perhaps, think of detachment or involvement as *necessary* prerequisites for fruitful scientific work. Most certainly, one cannot test the validity of scientific propositions by investigating the scientist's detachment or involvement. Detachment and involvement, are not methodological "devices"; they are, instead, psychological attributes. But even though the scientist's psychology is irrelevant for determining the validity of his findings, it is of undeniable importance as one of the factors determining the very aims and methods of his investigations.
2. "Eshchë odno unichtozhenie sotsializma," in *Sochineniia*, XVII, 272.
3. *Ludwig Feuerbach*, pp. 68–69. Cf. also *The Peasant War*, p. 27.
4. *The Poverty of Philosophy*, p. 106.
5. *Anti-Dühring*, p. 355.
6. Marx, *Zur Kritik der politischen Ökonomie*, Vorwort, p. xlviii.
7. *Die deutsche Ideologie*, p. 60.
8. Cf. the Theses on Feuerbach, where Marx writes that "the philosophers have only interpreted the world. The important thing, however, is to change it." Marx himself would have been the first to admit that this is a denial of all philosophy in the traditional sense, though he thought that this denial was more like a Hegelian negation: The unity of philosophy and political action was thought to be the synthesis which both abolished and preserved philosophy. As long as they remained contradictory, theory and action could only frustrate each other; they had to merge before either could be realized. In spite of major differences in

method and outlook, this aim of merging theory and practice has close affinities to both Pragmatism and Existentialism.

9. *Kritik der Hegelschen Rechtsphilosophie,* in Marx and Engels, *Historisch-kritische Gesamtausgabe,* I, 613, 615.

10. Marx, *Zur Kritik der Hegelschen Rechtsphilosophie,* in *Frühschriften,* p. 17.

11. Karl Korsch, *Marxismus und Philosophie* (Leipzig: C. L. Hirschfeld, 1930), p. 148.

Chapter 5: Marxism as Ideology

1. In one of his earlier works, he even hints that ideas are more important than other "material" forces: "We are firmly convinced that not the *practical attempt* but the *theoretical* [*development*] of Communist ideas constitutes the real *danger* [to the present order]; for practical *attempts, though they be attempts by the masses,* can be answered by cannons, but *ideas* which our intelligence battles successfully, which our whole outlook conquers, to which reason forges our conscience, — they are chains which we cannot tear off without tearing our hearts to pieces, they are demons which man can conquer only by submitting to them." *Frühschriften,* p. 202.

2. "The proletariat has fought against capitalism by forcing bourgeois society to become so conscious of itself that by inescapable logic this society had to appear problematic in its very core." Lukács, *Geschichte und Klassenbewusstsein,* p. 234.

3. Marx, Letter to Ruge, 1843. In Marx and Engels, *Über historischen Materialismus,* Teil I, p. 14.

4. An interesting illustration is the importance which Engels attributed to the labor theory of value as a moral rallying cry for the proletariat. Both the so-called Utopian Socialists and Marx took as point of departure Ricardo's propositions, (1) that the value of any commodity is solely determined by the quantity of labor required for its production; and (2) that the product of all social labor is divided among three classes: (a) landowners get rent; (b) capitalists get profit; and (c) workers get wages. Socialism, writes Marx, draws the following conclusion from this.

And Engels quotes from the *Critique of Political Economy:* "If the exchange value of a product is equal to the labor time which it contains, the exchange value of a labor day is equal to its product. Or the wage must be equal to the product of labor. But the contrary is the case."

But he adds the following note: "The theoretical correctness of the formula being presupposed, practice was blamed for contradiction with theory, and bourgeois society was invited to draw in practice the supposed conclusions from its theoretical principle. In this way at least, English socialists turned the Ricardian formula of exchange value against political economy.

Engels later commented on this in a very interesting fashion: "The above application of the Ricardian theory . . . leads directly to communism. But, as Marx indicates . . . formally it is economically incorrect, for it is simply an application of morality to economics. According to the laws of bourgeois economics, the greatest part of the product does *not* belong to the workers who have produced it. If we now say: that is unjust, that ought not to be so, then that has nothing immediately to do with economics. We are merely saying that this economic fact is in contradiction to our moral sentiment. Marx . . . never based his communist demands upon this, but upon the inevitable collapse of the capitalist mode of production which is taking place daily before our eyes to an increasing degree; he says only that surplus value consists of unpaid labor, which is a simple fact.

"But what formally may be economically incorrect may all the same be correct from the point of view of world history. If the *moral consciousness of the masses* declares an economic fact to be unjust, as it has done in the cases of slavery or serf labor, that is proof that the fact itself has been out-lived, that other economic facts have made their appearance, owing to which the former has become unbearable and untenable. Therefore, a very true economic content may be concealed behind the formal economic incorrectness." Engels, Preface to the first German edition of *Das Elend der Philosophie* (*The Poverty of Philosophy*), p. 10. (Italics added.)

5. Professor Herbert Butterfield's essay on Marxist historiography is one of the most thoughtful and at the same time one of the strongest of such statements. *History and Human Relations* (London: William Collins Sons & Co., 1951), pp. 66–100.

6. Marx and Engels, *Manifesto of the Communist Party.* (London: Lawrence and Wishart, 1946) p. 38.

7. There are a number of statements in the writings of Marx and Engels to the effect that the proletariat might come to power in a legal, constitutional way. For instance, in his critique of the Erfurt program of 1891 Engels mentions the possibility of such a constitutional revolution for the United States, England and France. It is noteworthy, however, that he does so in order to contrast these Western democracies against Germany where, he writes, constitutional illusions should be curbed because the German constitution is no more than the "fig leaf that hides the shame of absolutism" (*Kritik des Sozial-demokratischen Programm-Entwurfes,* pp. 63–67). Again, there is an oft-quoted passage in his introduction to Marx's *Class Struggles in France,* where Engels writes that, after the repeal of the antisocialist laws in Germany, the proletarian has become the first champion of democracy. Revolution now thrives better on legal methods than the bourgeois liberals themselves. This in turn tempts the bourgeoisie

to break its own rules. But here Engels invokes the political contract and says that, as the ruling classes begin to repress the people, the old right to make revolution reverts to the proletariat. *Class Struggles in France* (New York: International Publishers, 1935), p. 27. See also note 19 of this chapter.

8. Engels, essay on the "ten hour bill," in *Neue Rheinische Zeitung,* Heft 4.

9. Cf. Solomon F. Bloom, *The World of Nations* (New York: Columbia University Press 1941), *passim.*

10. Spoken in September, 1850. Quoted in Marx, *Enthüllungen über den Kommunistenprozess zu Köln* (2nd ed.; Hottingen-Zürich: Volksbuchhandlung, 1885), p. 21.

11. Marx, letter to Kugelman, 1870.

12. From a draft for the Communist Manifesto written by Engels in 1847. Marx and Engels, *Historisch-Kritische Gesamtausgabe,* Sec. I, vol. 6, p. 516.

13. *Capital,* I, 533.

14. *Ibid.,* p. 482.

15. Lest the point made in the preceding pages concerning the steadily widening gap between the maximal and the minimal programs become an overstatement, it should be made clear that this distinction was already made in the Communist Manifesto. Its significance in this document, however, is considerably diminished by the immediacy with which the revolution of 1848 was expected and by the confidence that this bourgeois revolution would transform itself directly into a proletarian revolution. Naturally, the gap became even wider when the expectation of bourgeois revolution diminished, as it did in underdeveloped countries.

16. Bernstein, *Die Voraussetzungen des Sozialismus und die Aufgaben der Sozialdemokratie* (Stuttgart: Dietz, 1899), p. 128.

17. In decrying the growth of the party bureaucracy, Luxemburg and others fought not only Lenin and his Russian Bolsheviks, but also the leaders of the German Social-Democratic Party, from whom Lenin learned some of his principles of organization in the first place.

18. Controversies over the nature, aims, organization, and other aspects of the general strike rocked the German Social-Democratic Movement in the last decade of the nineteenth and the first of the twentieth centuries and served, incidentally, to break one of the best friendships in the movement, that between Rosa Luxemburg and Karl Kautsky. For the polemical literature produced in the course of this controversy, see the following: Karl Kautsky, *Der politische Massenstreik* (Berlin: Paul Singer Verlag, 1914); "Allerhand Revolutionäres," in *Neue Zeit,* XXII, 1; "Literarische Rundschau," *ibid.,* XXIII, 1; "Eine neue Strategie," *ibid.,* XXVIII, 2; "Zwischen Baden und Luxemburg," *ibid.,* XXVIII, 2; and "Schlusswort," *ibid.,* XXVIII, 2. Rosa Luxemburg, *Massenstreik, Partei und Gewerkschaften* (Hamburg: Verlag Erdmann-Dubber, 1906), cf. also *Neue Zeit,*

XXII, 1; "Das belgische Experiment," *Neue Zeit*, XX, 2; "Ermattung oder Kampf?," *ibid.*, XXVIII, 2; "Die Theorie und Praxis," *ibid.*, XXVIII, 2; "Zur Richtigstellung," *ibid.*, XXVIII, 2. Rudolf Hilferding, "Zur Frage des Generalstreikes," *Neue Zeit*, 1903. Eduard Bernstein, "Der Streik als politisches Kampfmittel," *ibid.*, XII, 1. "Parvus," "Staatsstreich und politischer Massenstreik," *ibid.*, XIV, 2. Michael Lusnia, "Unbewaffnete Revolution?," *ibid.*, XXII, 1. Franz Mehring, "Historisch-Materialistische Literatur," *ibid.*, XXV, 2; "Die sicherste Politik," *ibid.*, XXVIII, 1. Henriette Roland-Holst, *Generalstreik und Sozialdemokratie* (Dresden: Kaden & Co., 1905–06).

19. Friedrich Engels, "Denkschrift über den Aufstand in Spanien im Sommer 1873," quoted in Karl Kautsky, *Der politische Massenstreik*, pp. 17–18. Another passage which reflects the inability, particularly of Engels, to make up his mind concerning the possibility of a proletarian dictatorship established by legal, constitutional methods, occurs in the preface he wrote to the first English translation of *Capital*. Engels here points out that Marx was "led to the conclusion that, at least in Europe, England is the only country where the inevitable social revolution might be effected entirely by peaceful and legal means. He certainly never forgot to add that he hardly expected the English ruling classes to submit, without a 'pro-slavery rebellion,' to this peaceful and legal revolution." *Capital*, I, 32. The reader has doubtless noticed that, in the second sentence, Engels takes back all that he has admitted in the first.

Chapter 6: The Marxist House Divided

1. *Evolutionary Socialism*, p. 79.

2. *Ibid.*, pp. 52–54.

3. *Ibid.*, pp. 142–3.

4. *Ibid.*, pp. xiii–xiv.

5. *Ibid.*, p. 12. The ideological development sketched here was by no means confined to Germany, even though our illustrations are taken from discussions originating in that country. As a matter of fact, revisionists had adherents everywhere, even in Russia. Socialists like Jaurès and Millerand for instance, went further in their revision of Marxist ideas and Marxist politics than the German revisionists. Nevertheless, Bernstein is perhaps the clearest and most notable exponent of this school.

6. Max Eastman, *Marxism, Is It Science?* (New York: W. W. Norton & Co., 1940), p. 114.

7. Rudolf Hilferding, *Finanzkapital* (Wien: Verlag der Wiener Volksbuchhandlung, 1910 and 1923), preface, p. x.

8. Lenin and his school not only learned their Marxism from Kautsky and other orthodox interpreters, joining them in their fight against revisionism, they also remained orthodox in their psychological make-up long

after Kautsky had made substantial compromises; and their ideas, their points of emphasis, and their blind spots are often the same as those of the "orthodox" discussed here.

9. For similar reasons, the orthodox Stalin faction could not swallow the warnings of the left opposition and therefore had to condemn it as an ineffective myth. Said Stalin, "The essence of Trotskyism consists, first of all, in the denial of the possibility of building Socialism in the USSR with the forces of the working class and the peasantry of our country . . . This means that if, in the near future, a victorious world revolution does not hasten to our help, we shall have to capitulate to the bourgeoisie and clear the road for a bourgeois-democratic republic. Consequently, we have here the bourgeois repudiation of the possibility of building Socialism in our country, masked by 'revolutionary' phrase-mongering about the victory of the world revolution. *With such views, is it possible to inspire millions of workers with enthusiasm for work, to enlist them for socialist competition or for shock brigade work on a mass scale, to mobilize them for an all-out offensive against capitalist elements?* Clearly, this would be impossible. It would be foolish to think that our working class, after having made three revolutions, would become enthusiastic about work and shock brigade work on a mass scale only for the purpose of manuring the soil for capitalism. Our working class takes on its labors not for the sake of capitalism but for the purpose of burying capitalism once and for all times and building Socialism in the USSR. Deprive them of their confidence in the possibility of building Socialism, and you will destroy every possible basis for competition, for labor enthusiasm, for the shock brigade movement. Hence it follows that in order to raise the working class's enthusiasm for work, stimulate competition and organize an all-out offensive, we must, first of all, bury the bourgeois theory of Trotskiism concerning the impossibility of building Socialism in our country." Stalin, Political report of the Central Committee to the XVIth Party Congress, *Sochineniia,* XII, 354–5. (Italics added.)

10. *Evolutionary Socialism,* p. 212.

11. See p. 140.

12. Frequently this was stated with reservations; either that Marxism had been the last word in social science in its day, or else it was argued that even though the revisionists were right in rejecting certain philosophical features of Marx's and Engels' theories, Marxism as a social theory could still be accepted. Kautsky, for one, came to hold that Marxism as a social science was compatible with various philosophies.

13. *Materialistische Geschichtsauffassung* (Berlin: Dietz, 1929), I 128–154.

14. Vortwort zu Marx, *Inauguraladresse* (Stuttgart: Dietz, 1922), p. 15.

15. At the same time, she enthusiastically hailed the Russian revolution of 1905, arguing that the sluggish and bureaucratized Marxist movement in the West could learn from the revolutionary movement in backward countries. Her idea that the backward countries, just because they are

late-comers, may show the advanced societies the way by which to break out of the past, is very close to the views of Lenin and Trotsky. Moreover, Luxemburg's conception of the class struggle as something international par excellence was closely tied with her theory of imperialism. Kautsky, thinking in terms of Western Europe, described the Russian revolution as a perversion of the Marxist pattern; Luxemburg seemed to hail it as a strong blow against the world system of capitalist imperialism.

16. At the same time Karl Kautsky was well on his way to "returning to Kant." For one thing, he now held that materialism meant nothing else than scientific method, the usage of the term by Marx being explained as a reaction against Hegel; secondly, he now maintained that Marxism, as social science, was compatible with several philosophies, including neo-Kantianism.

17. See John Kautsky, "The Political Thought of Karl Kautsky; a Theory of Democratic, Anti-Communist Marxism," Harvard thesis, 1951, *passim.*

18. Kautsky, *Die proletarische Revolution und ihr Program* (Berlin und Stuttgart: Dietz, 1922), p. 196.

Chapter 7: Conclusion

1. For a useful elaboration of some of these ideas, see Donald G. MacRae, "The Bolshevik Ideology," in *The Cambridge Journal,* V, 3 (December 1951), pp. 164–177.

2. *Anti-Dühring,* p. 90.

Bibliography

The function of a bibliography is to guide the reader toward further studies of the subject matter discussed in the book. The ideal bibliography therefore is not merely a list of titles, but an annotated, critical guide to the significant literature in the field. Any attempt to write such a guide in the present case would be a hopeless undertaking, for a number of reasons. To begin with, an exhaustive bibliography of works by Marx and Engels alone would almost be of book length. Furthermore, Marxism is a world view, or has turned into one. Although it was conceived as an analysis of modern industrial civilization, its origins, functioning, problems, and trends of development, most followers of Marx have sought to widen the scope of its applicability. In their hands, Marxism has turned into a universal science of man, nature, and the universe. From literary criticism to biology, from theories of the business cycle to theories of knowledge, there is hardly a field of learning in which conflicting Marxist schools of interpretation have not been developed. An adequate bibliography of Marxism would therefore not only swell to voluminous proportions; it would also be bewilderingly diverse.

In addition, Marxism is a political movement. The development of Marxist thought is intimately bound up with the changing political constellation, and with the strategy worked out by Marxist leaders on the basis of both ideas and political conditions. Hence an exhaustive bibliography on Marxism would have to include the literature which discusses its political history. Finally, we must consider the fact that Marxism has aroused incessant controversy, carried on by adherents, friends, critics, and bystanders, who represent a confusing variety of viewpoints. An honest bibliography would have to be careful to have all the important views represented. This is a formidable task to which no modest selection, say, of a hundred works, could do justice.

Given this vast amount of literature, the best advice that might be given to interested readers is, probably, that they should turn first of all to the writings of Marx and Engels themselves. Here too any selection would be arbitrary and misleading.* This applies particularly for readers un-

---

* The works customarily selected as the best introductions to Marx or one of his followers are not always well chosen. Thus *Anti-Dühring*, by Engels, is a shallow and highly controversial popularization of Marxist principles; its importance for an understanding of these principles is negligble. And no single work could be as untypical of Lenin's thought as the book customarily picked as his most important work, *The State and Revolution*.

familiar with German. For some of the most important works of Marx and Engels have not yet been translated into other Western languages.

Our advice to the reader who is unacquainted with the writings of Marx and Engels is therefore to plunge into them, beginning with whatever works he might find available. There are some useful anthologies which might serve as a starter. The purpose for which such a reader would take up these works would be to familiarize himself with the language of Marx and to have an impression of his way of arguing.

The student who wishes to study Marxist writings systematically had best consult the collected works of Marx and Engels, which have been published by the Marx-Engels Institute, in Moscow. The German edition of this *Historisch-Kritische Gesamtausgabe* (customarily cited as *MEGA*) is not complete; the Russian edition is said to be complete, although a careful comparison of this translation with previous publications would doubtless reveal significant omissions.

The works of Marx and Engels should be complemented by the works of their most important followers, such as Adler, Bauer, Bernstein, Kautsky, Lenin, Luxemburg, and Plekhanov, to name only a few of them at random. Their writings, too, are of impressive volume. Lenin's collected works, for instance, fill thirty sizeable tomes, which can be supplemented by a vast collection of unpublished drafts, notes, and other Leniniana, which comprise a little library shelf of their own. Finally, since Marxism is best understood, perhaps, as an "ideological reflexion" of the modern world, the student of its ideas would do well to supplement this reading by familiarizing himself as much as possible with the social and political history of the last hundred-odd years.

The following list might serve as a brief vade mecum for readers who, having been introduced to Marx, would like to go further.

1. Anthologies

Burns, Emile. (ed.). *A Handbook of Marxism*. New York: International Publishers, n. d. Includes selections from the writings of Lenin and Stalin.

Marx, Karl. *Selected Works*. 2 vol. New York: International Publishers, 1936–1937.

2. Selection of works by Marx and Engels available in English

Marx, Karl. *Capital*. 3 vol. Chicago: C. H. Kerr & Co., 1906, 1909, 1933.

———. *The Class Struggles in France*. New York: International Publishers, 1934.

———. *The Civil War in France*. New York: International Publishers, 1933.

———. *Contribution to the Critique of Political Economy*. Chicago: C. H. Kerr & Co., 1911.

———. *Critique of the Gotha Program*. New York: International Publishers, 1936.

————. *The Eighteenth Brumaire of Louis Bonaparte.* New York: International Publishers, 1926.

————. *The Poverty of Philosophy.* Chicago: C. H. Kerr & Co., 1910.

————. *Selected Essays.* New York: International Publishers, 1926.

ENGELS, FRIEDRICH. *The Condition of the Working Class in England in 1844.* London: G. Allen & Unwin, 1926.

————. *Germany, Revolution and Counter-revolution.* New York: International Publishers, 1933.

————. *Herr Eugen Dühring's Revolution in Science.* New York: International Publishers, 1935.

————. *Ludwig Feuerbach and the Outcome of Classical German Philosophy.* New York: International Publishers, n. d.

————. *The Origin of the Family, Private Property, and the State.* Chicago: C. H. Kerr & Co., 1905.

————. *The Peasant War in Germany.* New York: International Publishers, 1926.

MARX, KARL, and FRIEDRICH ENGELS, *Correspondence: A Selection.* New York: International Publishers, 1936.

————. *The German Ideology.* Parts I and III only. New York: International Publishers, 1939.

————. *Manifesto of the Communist Party.* New York: International Publishers. Several editions.

3. *Selected works by followers and critics of Marx in English*

ADAMS, H. P. *Karl Marx and his Earlier Writings.* London: G. Allen & Unwin, 1940.

BERLIN, ISAIAH. *Karl Marx.* New York: Oxford University Press, 1948.

BERNSTEIN, EDUARD. *Evolutionary Socialism.* New York: Huebsch, 1911.

BLOOM, S. F. *The World of Nations.* New York: Columbia University Press, 1941.

BOUDIN, B. *The Theoretical System of Karl Marx.* Chicago: C. H. Kerr & Co., 1907.

BUKHARIN, N. I. *Historical Materialism.* New York: International Publishers, 1925.

————. *Imperialism and World Economy.* New York: International Publishers, 1929.

CARR, E. H. *Karl Marx: A Study in Fanaticism.* London: J. M. Dent & Sons, 1934.

COLE, G. D. H. *The Meaning of Marxism.* London: V. Gollancz, 1948.

CROCE, BENEDETTO. *Historical Materialism and the Economics of Karl Marx.* New York: The Macmillan Co., 1914.

EASTMAN, MAX. *Marx and Lenin: the Science of Revolution.* London: G. Allen & Unwin, 1926.

————. *Marxism: Is It a Science?* New York: W. W. Norton & Co., 1940.

HILFERDING, RUDOLF. *Böhm von Bawerk's Criticism of Marx,* together with EUGEN BÖHM von BAWERK, *Karl Marx and the Close of his System.* New York: Augustus M. Kelley, 1949.

HOOK, SIDNEY. *From Hegel to Marx.* New York: Reynal & Hitchcock, 1926.

———. *Toward the Understanding of Karl Marx.* New York: John Day, 1933.

KAUTSKY, KARL. *The Dictatorship of the Proletariat.* London: International Labour Press, 1919.

———. *The Economic Doctrines of Karl Marx.* New York: The Macmillan Co., 1936.

———. *Ethics and the Materialist Conception of History.* Chicago: C. H. Kerr & Co., 1918.

KORSCH, KARL. *Karl Marx.* New York: J. Wiley & Sons, 1938.

LENIN, V. I. *Collected Works.* New York: International Publishers, 1927–19—. Only a small number of volumes of this edition, which is a translation of the second Russian edition of Lenin's works, has appeared.

———. *Selected Works.* 12 vol. New York: International Publishers, 1943.

———. *Marx, Engels, Marxism.* Moscow: Foreign Language Publishing House, 1947. This is a handy one-volume anthology.

LUXEMBURG, ROSA. *The Accumulation of Capital.* New York: Yale University Press, 1951.

The Crisis in the German Social Democracy. New York. Socialist Publication Society. 1919.

MAYER, GUSTAV. *Friedrich Engels.* New York: A. A. Knopf, 1936.

MEHRING, FRANZ. *Karl Marx.* London: G. Allen & Unwin, 1936.

PLEKHANOV, G. V. *Art and Social Life.* London: Lawrence & Wishart, 1953.

———. *Fundamental Problems of Marxism.* New York: International Publishers, n. d.

———. *In Defense of Materialism.* London: Lawrence & Wishart, 1947.

POPPER, K. R. *The Open Society and Its Enemies.* Princeton: Princeton University Press, 1950.

ROBINSON, JOAN. *An Essay on Marxian Economics.* London: Macmillan & Co., 1942.

ROSENBERG, ARTHUR. *A History of Bolshevism.* London: Oxford University Press, 1934.

SCHLESINGER, RUDOLF. *Marx: His Time and Ours.* London: Routledge & Paul, 1950.

SWEEZY, PAUL M. *The Theory of Capitalist Development.* New York: Oxford University Press, 1942.

VENABLE, VERNON. *Human Nature: the Marxist View.* New York: A. A. Knopf, 1946.

WILSON, EDMUND. *To The Finland Station.* New York: Harcourt, Brace & Co., 1940.

Index

RUSSIAN RESEARCH CENTER STUDIES

* Out of print.
† Publications of the Harvard Project on the Soviet Social System.
‡ Published jointly with the Center for International Affairs, Harvard University.